Physical Cha...
Wels...
(from The Kenn...

Tail: Well set on but not carried too gaily.

Body: Back short and well ribbed up, loin strong, good depth and moderate width of chest.

Hindquarters: Strong, thighs muscular, of good length, with hocks well bent, well let down and with ample bone.

Colour: Black and tan for preference, or black grizzle and tan, free from black pencilling on toes.

Size: Height at shoulder not exceeding 39 cms (15.5 ins). Weight: 9–9.5 kgs (20–21 lbs).

Feet: Small, round and cat-like.

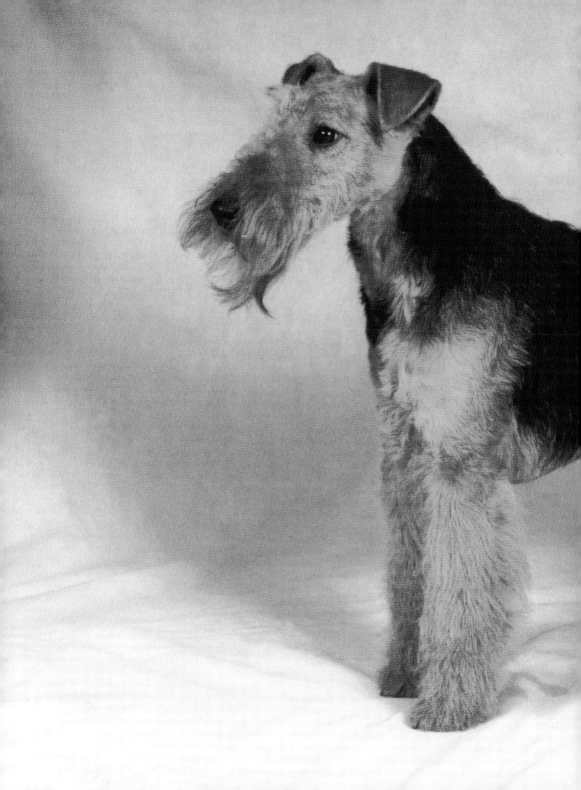

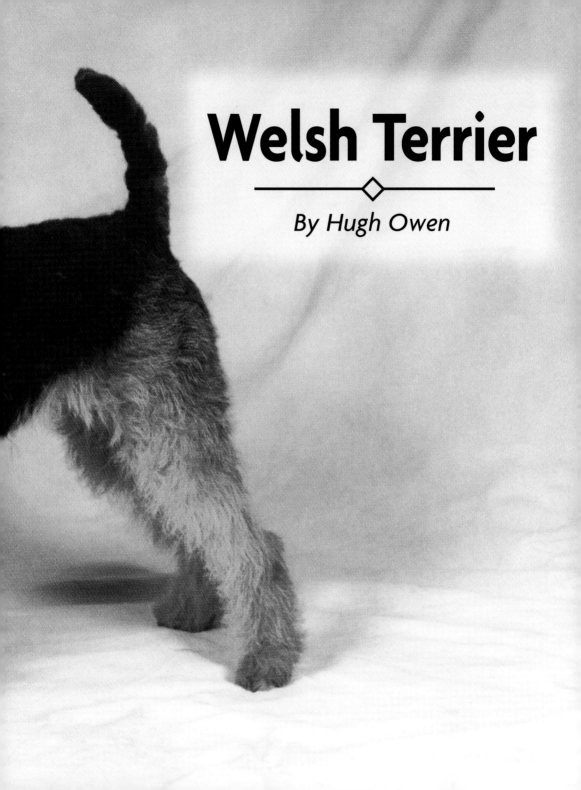

Welsh Terrier

◇

By Hugh Owen

Contents

PUBLISHED IN THE UNITED KINGDOM BY:

INTERPET
PUBLISHING

Vincent Lane, Dorking, Surrey RH4 3YX England

ISBN 1-903098-83-1

Photography by Carol Ann Johnson and Michael Trafford with additional photographs by:

Norvia Behling, TJ Calhoun, Carolina Biological Supply, Doskocil, Isabelle Francais, James Hayden-Yoav, James R Hayden, RBP, Bill Jonas, Dwight R Kuhn, Dr Dennis Kunkel, Bardi McLennan, Mikki Pet Products, Phototake, Jean Claude Revy and Dr Andrew Spielman.

Illustrations by Patricia Peters.

The publisher wishes to thank all of the owners whose dogs are illustrated in this book, including Ms Wendy Allen, Judy Averis, Mereda Cornick, Gillian Griffiths, Mrs Kelles, Mr Juha Korhonen, Sari Mäkelä, Anne Maughan, Cathleen Saito, Dave Scawthorn, Kim Skillman and Linda Taranto.

Glansevin Coquette and Ch Glansevin Coda, in a painting from 1907, illustrate quality Welsh Terrier type of that time.

History of the
WELSH TERRIER

THE WELSH TERRIER ORIGINAL

There are no written pedigrees before the 1800s for the small black and tan terriers bred by Celtic farmers, but clear references to them, including their monetary value (three curt pence), can be found in writings from as early as the 10th century. The dogs, like their owners, worked in the soil, hence the name 'terrier,' taken from the Latin *terra,* meaning earth. These small dogs helped rid the farms of all forms of vermin from mice to marten, and provided an occasional rabbit for the dinner table. They were true workers and when their job was done, they had earned the right to relax by the fire with the family. Thus a sensible temperament has always been intrinsic to the breed: sensible and single-minded working in the fields or alone underground; agreeable working with other dogs; steady and reliable in the home.

When it was found that fox hunting benefited from the addition of terriers to the packs of hounds in order to bolt the fox, the terriers' worth was raised a notch. However, it was due to the rapid expansion of dog shows that the Welsh Terrier gained popularity and prestige in the Terrier Group and became the handsome dog we have today. An opposing view holds that dog shows have put the cart before the horse by placing the emphasis on conformation and looks rather than on intelligence and working ability. Fortunately, this is not true in all countries.

In the beginning, the Welsh Terrier was little known outside its Celtic environs, which, at one time, went far beyond the boundaries of Wales as we know it today, encompassing a portion of the Continent and stretching into present-day Scotland and England. It is based on this historical fact that many in the breed feel so strongly that the breed eventually named the Welsh Terrier was indeed the progenitor of the other black and tan terriers inhabiting the British Isles.

Around 1450 a Welsh thank-you note (*Englyn diolgarwch*) was written, acknowledging the gift of a terrier. It reads in part,

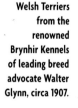

Welsh Terriers from the renowned Brynhir Kennels of leading breed advocate Walter Glynn, circa 1907.

> **DOGS AS LIFE**
> The old Celtic religion used dogs as symbols of healing, death and rebirth. Apparently the Celtic canine was sufficiently regarded to cover all aspects of life.

'And a good black and red terrier bitch to choke the brown polecat and to tear up the red fox.' It is quite possibly the earliest written description of the Welsh Terrier—a dog that was black and tan (the same 'red' as a fox) and a worker of note.

The breed was known to have been used with the Glansevin Welsh Hounds from the early 1600s, and records of 1760 show that these terriers had also been used for several generations by the Jones family with their Ynysfor Otterhounds.

WHAT'S IN A NAME?
In the first dog shows where Welsh Terriers were exhibited, the classes were all-inclusive, for example, 'Working Terriers'

or 'Any Variety Terriers.' The individual naming of each breed occurred with the increase in dog shows and the establishment of The Kennel Club in 1873. In the case of the Welsh Terrier, The Kennel Club was to become the arena for conflicting national canine contentions to do battle!

The Welsh had always considered the black and tans as their very own, referred to as *daeargi*, of course, not as Welsh Terriers. The English now laid claim to their version as the taproot of the breed under several elongated names such as the Old English Broken-Haired Black and Tan Terrier or the Old English Wire-Haired Black and Tan Terrier. So it was that The Kennel Club had an international crisis of sorts on their hands.

A decisive event had taken place a year before in Pwllheli, North Wales: the first show with separate classes for Welsh Terriers, a speciality, if you will. On 28 August 1884, at the Lleyn

GENUS *CANIS*
Dogs and wolves are members of the genus *Canis*. Wolves are known scientifically as *Canis lupus* while dogs are known as *Canis domesticus*. Dogs and wolves are known to interbreed. The term *canine* derives from the Latin-derived word *Canis*. The term 'dog' has no scientific basis but has been used for thousands of years. The origin of the word 'dog' has never been authoritatively ascertained.

& Eifionydd Agricultural Show, two highly regarded elderly Welshmen, who had bred these terriers for many years, were asked to judge an entry of 90 dogs, divided into three classes. Mr Griffith Owen and Mr Humphrey Griffith spent the entire day going over the dogs one at a time, each being judged on its own merits, not compared to any other dog. It is said that all were pleased with the results, which today in itself might be considered something of a miracle!

ACTION!
In these early years, Welsh Terriers were most numerous in North Wales, and it was said that

WELSH GRAMMAR LESSON
The Welsh alphabet does not include the letters K, J, Q, V, X or Z, but it does have six others to make up for it. It goes like this: A, B, C, CH, D, E, F, FF, G, H, I, (J only for words borrowed from English), L, LL, M, N, O, P, PH, R, RH, S, T, TH, U, W and Y.

Cledwyn Owen, William Jones and Price O Pughe knew all the Welsh Terriers in the area as well as their pedigrees. By 1885, Welsh terriermen (including Owen, Jones and Pughe) had had enough of the name nonsense and with nine others formed The Welsh Terrier Club. They were recognised by The Kennel Club in 1886, whereupon, in what can only be described as an act of diplomacy, The Kennel Club provided classes for both the Welsh Terriers and the Old English Broken-Haired Black and Tan Terriers (OEBHBTT). However, that was not to be the end of the story. Things began to fall apart for the Old English supporters, who never were able to put together an organisation to back them. Nor did their dogs help matters.

For two years, 1885 and 1886, no OEBHBTT shown was from the mating of an OEBHBTT sire and dam. All were first-generation cross-breds. The dogs were said, in general, to be somewhat more handsome than

STAND BACK, PATAGONIA!
It is now fashionable, especially among the young, to speak Welsh in Patagonia, an area of Argentina originally settled by the Welsh in the 1800s. Teachers have been sent there by the Welsh Office in Britain with an added plum for the students—six annual scholarships to study Welsh in Wales.

the Welsh Terrier, but since they were manufactured and could not reproduce in kind, this alone would seem to give credibility to the Welsh Terrier as the generic black and tan. It should be noted that in those days there was no Kennel Club ruling against cross-breeding, but serious breeders in the new sport of dog shows wanted pure-bred stock.

The results during those two years bordered on breed chaos, for many dogs were shown—and declared winners—in both classes. For example, one dog named Crib was shown as an OEBHBTT, but had been sired by a well-known Smooth Fox Terrier out of a solid black rough-coated bitch. He was also known to be deaf, a fault that the judges of the day apparently chose to overlook.

A dog named Dick Turpin was also famous for being caught in the middle of the dispute. The dog was Welsh-bred, but

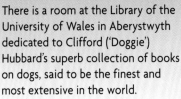

DOGGIE HUBBARD LIVES ON
There is a room at the Library of the University of Wales in Aberystwyth dedicated to Clifford ('Doggie') Hubbard's superb collection of books on dogs, said to be the finest and most extensive in the world.

changed owners four times. Each owner was apparently unsure where to enter the dog, so Dick was entered in both OEBHBTT and Welsh Terrier classes. The show results proved his heritage because he only won a first place when shown as a Welsh Terrier.

AND THE WINNER IS . . .

The Kennel Club ended the battle, and on 5 April 1887 dropped the Old English, etc., leaving the Welsh Terrier as the only recognised breed. One has to wonder if the long, clumsy OEBHBTT name may have influenced The Kennel Club's decision.

It should be noted that the Welsh Terriers entered in these early shows were, for the most part, a far cry from the beautiful dogs we see in the ring today. They were still primarily working terriers and meant to look the part. Cropped ears, for example, were allowed since terriers' ears were often ripped by prey. The breed was not yet

---

WELSH ROOTS AT BULLDOG UNIVERSITY

Elihu Yale, founder of Yale University in New Haven, Connecticut, had close ties to Wales. His family was from Plas-yn-Ial and although Elihu was born in America (where the spelling of the family name was changed from Ial to Yale), he retained his Welsh roots to the end and is buried in St. Giles Churchyard in Wrexham. As an acknowledgement of this association, a replica of the St. Giles tower stands at the University.

---

consistent in size or type. Many dogs had unattractive broad heads, drooping ears and white feet. The looks of the scruffy working terrier improved when popular opinion demanded it. The fashionable Wire Fox Terrier was what the public admired, and no doubt crosses with the Welsh were made to it. Judging from existing photographs, quite a few of these early dogs would be considered satisfactory breed specimens today.

EARLY SHOW DOGS

At the Bangor show in 1887, a bitch appropriately named Bangor Dau Lliw (Bangor Two Colours) became the first Welsh Terrier bitch champion. She was bred and owned by Mr Dew. At this same show, Walter Glynn, who was to become the leading

---

A PINT FOR BEST OF BREED?

Some of the first gatherings of dog owners, the precursors of today's dog shows, took place in pubs. Everyone in the pub became judge, exhibitor and spectator, all going over the dogs and giving their opinions.

Ch Vaynor Again, a male Welsh Terrier born in 1928.

advocate of the breed, exhibited his first Welsh Terrier, a puppy dog named Dim Saesonaeg (No English). Bred by Mr R O Pughe, the dog was made up a champion in 1889. He was highly regarded in his day. However, his son Ch Cymro-o-Gymry (The Welshman from Wales) became the leading light of the breed. Bred by J Mitchell out of Mitchell's bitch Blink Bonny in 1891, Cymro won 27 Challenge Certificates and for

Ch What's Wanted caused a sensation when she appeared on the show scene as a puppy during the 1919-1920 season. Her debut was followed by a brilliant show career.

many years was thought to be the embodiment of something close to perfection in the breed.

The first dog champion was made up in 1887. Mawddwy Nonsuch, sired by Fernyhurst Crab, was said to be a dog with an excellent head, albeit with cropped ears. Nonsuch was purchased by Edmund Buckley (Master of Otterhounds in Merioneth) for what was at the time the huge sum of 200 guineas. Possibly due in part to this extravagant expenditure, or the fact that the dog was said to lack type, doubts spread regarding the authenticity of the dog's dam. The gossip may well have been true since apparently he was never used at stud. Ch Bob Bethesda, a dog of Buckley's own breeding, was made up a champion soon after and was highly acclaimed as a show dog and for his excellent temperament.

The breed was gaining much attention throughout Wales, as well it might for this was also a period of intense Welsh national pride. As the number of dog shows increased and the dogs proved themselves winners in competition, the popularity of the breed increased at a rapid rate throughout the British Isles. Welsh Terriers were well represented in large shows such as Crystal Palace, Crufts and Birmingham. By 1896, Welsh

The Welsh Terrier as it appeared in an 1887 publication.

Terrier breeding and show stock was being exported in increasing numbers to Germany, Belgium, South Africa, India and America. Judges from the UK were much in demand to critique the progress of foreign breeding.

Two years after Walter Glynn purchased his first Welsh Terrier in 1887, he began judging Challenge classes at home and abroad and became a member of The Kennel Club. Dogs with his Brynhir affix became the foundation of many kennels worldwide. When he died in 1933, he had owned and bred more Welsh Terrier champions than anyone else in the previous half-century.

Another breeder of note on both sides of the Atlantic was T H Harris of Sennybridge, whose first Ch Resiant was made up in 1895. The first champion he actually owned and made up was Nell Gwynne in 1897. His Senny affix became synonymous with top-quality Welsh Terriers.

The first woman to award Challenge Certificates to Welsh Terriers was Mrs H L Aylmer in 1907 at the Bristol show. It is historically significant that she was chosen for this honour since her affix, Glansevin, came from her family ties with the Glansevin Welsh Hound Pack, noted for the Welsh Terriers that ran with it in the 1700s.

It should be noted that many Welsh Terriers in 1900 were still working terriers. By no means

Galen Rexus,
bred and owned
by Mr J S Gilbert,
was born in
September 1930.

Kynan O' Gaint
was Mr A T
Morris' dog, born
in March 1930.

had they given up their day jobs for stardom! The ownership of all dogs as pets had only become acceptable and popular due to the example set by Queen Victoria. Prior to that time, royalty carried about various toy breeds, but Everyman could not afford to feed a non-working animal. Dog shows took matters a step further. Those who could not afford to keep race horses, or horses and hounds for the hunt, could and did manage kennels of show dogs. Additionally, showing dogs held more prestige than showing livestock, although most of the early breeders had their roots in breeding sheep, rabbits or chickens to exhibit at agricultural shows. It may have been the idea that one could now take pride in selling a top show dog to a member of the aristocracy, whereas one could not hold one's head as high on the similar sale of a prize chicken!

In 1899, Princess Adolphus of Teck bought a bitch, Brynafon Nellie, and promptly became a breeder, exhibitor and ardent supporter of the Welsh Terrier Club. Then, in 1911, a group of Welsh Terrier fanciers in North Wales raised the necessary money and bought a dog for HRH The Prince of Wales. The rest of that story reads like pure fiction. The bitch was Queen Llechwedd (called Gwen), sired

Gochel Fi, owned by Mrs O Jones, was born in 1926. This fine Welsh Terrier beat three breed champions in the show ring.

by Dewi Sant (St. David, patron saint of Wales). The following year (1912) His Royal Highness registered two pups whelped on March first, St. David's Day. Serendipity continued to be on the side of the Welsh, although until the 1920s the controversy continued with articles referring to the 'so-called Welsh Terrier' and comparisons of the breed to the 'beautiful' Fox Terrier.

Not to worry. A new world

Ch Delswood Welcome, born in September 1931, was bred and owned by Mr A H Symonds.

Ch Lady Gwen, born in August 1925, earned her champion title at the National Terrier and Kennel Club Championship Shows. She was exported to Germany.

of dogs was on the rise and pets were becoming better fed, better housed and better cared for both at home and through outstanding advances in veterinary medicine.

THE WELSH GAINS FAME
Joe Hitchings' Aman kennels in the Rhondda Valley were a dominant force in the breed after

World War I and largely contributed to the area's being called 'the whelping box of the Welsh Terrier.' He handled many breeds, but is best remembered for putting a modern stamp on the Welsh Terrier. Hitchings, along with Sam Warburton in England and George Steadman Thomas (who was in effect a trans-Atlantic commuter) were responsible for a steady supply of quality Welsh Terriers to American kennels. With dogs being lined up on one side of the ocean and Welsh Terrier enthusiasts eagerly awaiting their arrival on the other, the stage was set for the breed's solid future in the modern world.

There were numerous true terriermen at this time. Hitchings continued breeding Welsh Terriers for 42 years. Arthur Harris (Ronvale), T H Harris (Senny) and A E Harris (Penhill) also remained in the breed for close to half a century. Harold Snow's Felstead kennels are to this day continued by his son Emlyn and grandson Lynn: three generations of dedication to the breed.

After World War II, the breed's popularity skyrocketed and names such as Mervin Pickering (Groveview), Dai Rees (Ebbw Swell), Cyril Williams (Caiach) and Phil Thomas (Sandstorm) came to the forefront. There were two presti-

Ch Senny Rex, owned by Mr T H Harris, was born in 1925.

gious wins in this period to boost the breed dramatically. The Crufts Best in Show winner in 1951 was Ch Twynstar Dyma Fi, and in 1959 Ch Sandstorm Saracen repeated the feat, handled by his breeder, Mr Thomas. It wasn't until 1994 that another Welsh Terrier was to claim the same honour, this time Ch Purston Hit and Miss From Brocolitia, bred by Michael Collings and owned by Mrs Anne J Maughan. The next Crufts Best in Show achievement followed just four years later, by Ch Saredon Forever Young, bred by Judy Averis and David Scawthorn.

Lord Atlee, former Prime Minister, chose his two Welsh Terriers as supporters for his coat of arms and the words *Labor omnia vincit* or 'Work conquers all'—a fitting tribute both to the man and the dogs. The Welsh fashion designer, Laura Ashley, bought a touch of fame to the breed when her Welsh Terrier, Clem, became the subject of a series of popular children's books.

Registration numbers in the UK were somewhat static until an high in 1927 of 288. By 1951, due in part to the fame of Twynstar Dyma Fi, those numbers escalated to 359. They remained in the 200–300 range, but new heights of popularity are expected in this 21st century.

Ch Bangor Dau Lliw was a record-breaking champion in the 1880s. In 1887, she became the first Welsh Terrier bitch champion.

In America the registrations average 700 annually.

There is always a threat to a breed such as the Welsh Terrier that inherited defects will become magnified in their small gene pool or that the overall quality will diminish. Fortunately for the breed, as import-export laws have been relaxed and the use of frozen

Ch Hold Up, owned by A E Harris, was born in 1925 and won many Challenge Certificates at important shows.

The larger Airedale Terrier is a breed closely related and very similar in looks to the Welsh Terrier.

semen increased, sound Welsh Terrier breeding stock is more easily obtainable world-wide.

A SECOND CLUB

In 1923, the Welsh Terrier Association (WTA) was founded in England, becoming the second club for the breed. The year prior, an older club, the South Wales Welsh Terrier Breeders' Association, which had been the breed's second club, joined up with The Welsh Terrier Club (WTC). A good portion of breed fanciers today belongs to both clubs. In 1970, WTA began a most informative and well-organised yearbook, reflecting the Welsh Terriers in Britain and in foreign lands. On 1 June 1980, this club held its first Open Show at the home of George and Olive Jackson (Jokyl), with 39 dogs in 88 entries. Judged by Beryl Blower

MADOC AT BAY

One of perhaps the wildest of Celtic claims concerned a Prince Madoc who was said to have crossed the Atlantic Ocean and landed in Mobile Bay, America in 1170. The legend was blessed by Queen Elizabeth in 1580, no doubt due in some large part to pressure from her Science Advisor and Magician, John Dee, who was—of course—a Welshman!

CHARLIE KENNEDY

Caroline Kennedy's Welsh Terrier, Charlie, swam in the White House pool with President John F Kennedy. Unfortunately, the dog was no diplomat—he lifted his leg indiscriminately, and so was confined to his quarters much of the time.

(Turith), Best in Show was awarded to Mr Jenkins' and Miss Nock's Ch Bowers Princess, handled by Ray Davies.

In 1981, when the Welsh Terrier Club was granted permission to award CCs, Mrs Margaret Thomas, Club President, was asked to judge the premier event. It is difficult to imagine why it took 95 years for The Kennel Club to acknowledge this stalwart club's standing; perhaps they never asked. The top Welsh Terrier that year and the following was Mr Jenkins' and Miss Nock's Ch Puzzle of Kenstaff, bred by R Ogles, a lovely bitch who won the Breed at Crufts and Best in Show at the National Terrier Speciality.

THE WORLD OF THE WELSH

In many countries on the Continent, dogs must still prove they can perform the tasks for which they were originally bred. As late as 1990 at the World

Although not as similar in looks, the Smooth Fox Terrier and the Welsh Terrier share many traits common to members of the Terrier Group.

Ch Vicway Live and Let Die, from Vicway kennel in Finland, winning Best in Show at the Terrier Club's Jubilee Show. Pictured with breeder-owner-handler Sari Mäkelä and Irish judge George O'Sullivan.

Show in Czechoslovakia, Welsh Terriers were a novelty as show dogs to people from Poland, Russia, Czechoslovakia and East Germany, but the breeders were charmed by the dogs' presence in the show ring and they are making great strides in that area. In Russia, a team of seven Welsh Terriers from Zo Strelki kennels won the Breeders Group at a show near Novgorod—and very nice specimens they were. Welsh

Terriers are still primarily working earthdogs in Russia, and in Poland they are actually the breed of choice for hunting.

GERMANY

The first classes for Welsh Terriers in Germany were at the Berlin show in 1896. Today the breed is in good shape with several dedicated breeders such as Mr Axel Mohrke, who has exported Bismarckquelle dogs world-wide. Mrs Irmatraud Becker (v. Ganseliesel) is another breeder with top-winning dogs.

DENMARK

Both the Borchorst and the El-Fri-Ba kennels are at the top of the breed in Denmark. Their Welsh Terrier stock has travelled as far as America and Australia.

A team from Russia's zo Strelki kennel, winning Best Breeders Group at the Novgorod, Russia show. Novgorod is home to several Welsh Terrier breeders, and interest in the breed is high in that area.

FINLAND

Registrations of the breed in Finland were on a downturn until quite recently. Due in great part to the success of Sari Mäkëla's Vicway dogs, things are looking up for the breed. Ch Vicway Live Free Or Die, a son of Multi-Ch Vicway Live and Let Die (a dog sired by Ch High Flyer's Welsh Baron), was a World Winner in 1998. Participation in agility has a slight edge over conformation shows.

WALES FOREVER!

In America's capital city, Washington, DC, half-way up the tall, cylindrical Washington Monument is inscribed *Cymru am bryth*—'Wales forever.'

SWEDEN

Sweden has been involved with the breed since dog shows began in that country. The late Per Thorsen (Snowdonia) played a leading role in establishing the popularity of the breed. Lars Adenheimer (Aden) is yet another Welsh Terrier breeder whose kennel affix is recognised everywhere.

The Swedish law against tail-docking not only has hurt the importing of dogs for the show ring but also has prevented Welsh Terriers with docked tails from competing in dog shows as well as agility, obedience or other such events. A recent World Show held in Sweden drew much criticism from owners of dogs that were disqualified for this reason,

Welsh Terriers on a winter walk in Finland with Jaana Matto.

Crufts winner, the successful Ch Purston Hit and Miss from Brocolitia.

when the docking of tails is still legal in their land of origin.

FRANCE

Mesdames Remy and Bernaudin of France owned the Best in Show Felstead Formulate and later purchased Ch Solentine Sugar Ray, a dog bred by Wendy Gatto-Ronchieri that was top stud dog in Britain in 1995.

HOLLAND

Holland is fortunate to have one of the world's top breeders, Jan Albers, whose High Flyer Welsh

Terriers have a definite stamp, a unique look. Many High Flyer dogs are top winners and producers and have been the foundation of other kennels on the Continent and overseas.

BRITAIN

Among the kennels of note today in the UK are Felstead, Philtown, Serenfach, Alokin, Davannadot, Saredon, Glyncastle and Wigmore. The breed is in excellent form in its native land with a steady growth of new breeders and exhibitors smitten by the Welsh Terrier.

MADE UP IN AMERICA

Not surprisingly, the largest population of Welsh Terriers today is in America and it all began when a young dog named Nigwood Nailer won a 30-guinea Challenge Cup for Best Welsh, Irish or Fox Terrier in Show in 1899 and was immediately bought up by Major Carnochan and taken to America. The following year, the Welsh Terrier Club of America was formed with Major Carnochan as Treasurer. Nigwood Nailer went on to become the first Welsh Terrier to be made up an American Kennel Club champion, which he did in 1903.

The Misses Beatrice and Gertrude de Coppet were to be the backbone of the club from 1900 until 1960. The sisters' Windermere kennels were among the first to be devoted solely to the Welsh Terrier, based on dogs imported from T H Harris in 1890. The ladies were always attired in hats and white kennel coats while handling their own dogs, and could be quite intimidating in the show ring. Among numerous contributions to the club, Beatrice de Coppet designed the club logo.

Over the ensuing years in America, many people and dogs established the Welsh Terrier as

Junior Handler winning an high award at an international Championship Show in Holland, under a judge from Florida, USA.

a worthy challenger in the Terrier Group. From the 1940s through the 1970s, kennel affixes such as Halcyon, Strathglass, Twin Ponds, Coltan, Pool Forge, Licken Run, Penzance and Tujays became staples of the breed. In more recent years, such names as Anasazi, Sunspryte, Hapitails, Kirkwood, Cisseldale and Czar are in the forefront. That is not to say the imports are lagging. They keep arriving and doing a fair share of winning.

USA RECORD BREAKERS

Three Welsh Terriers bred by Michael and Nancy O'Neal of New Mexico have each earned a place in the record books. Ch Anasazi Annie Oakley takes her place as top-winning Welsh Terrier bitch with 40 Bests in Show and 106 Terrier Group wins. Ch Anasazi Trail Boss topped the stud record with 60 champion get and Ch Anasazi Billy The Kid retired in 1999 after breaking all Welsh Terrier records with 100 Bests in Show and over 150 Group Firsts. An amazing feat from a small kennel!

> **BRAIN AND BRAWN**
> Since dogs have been inbred for centuries, their physical and mental characteristics are constantly being changed to suit man's desires for hunting, retrieving, scenting, guarding and warming their masters' laps. During the past 150 years, dogs have been judged according to physical characteristics as well as functional abilities. Few breeds can boast a genuine balance between physique, working ability and temperament.

The late Frank Kellett handled Ch Purston Hit and Miss from Brocolitia to Best in Show at Crufts in 1994. He is shown with owner Anne Maughan.

Characteristics of the
WELSH TERRIER

WHY THE WELSH TERRIER?
Sometimes one has to wonder if perchance the Welsh Terrier only speaks Welsh, for the dog has an uncanny knack of ignoring directions and commands given in the owner's native tongue. This is often mistaken for stubbornness, but that's not quite true. The Welsh Terrier is easily distracted and therefore may not be paying attention to you, or, more accurately, is paying strict attention to something else. That's the contradictory nature of the Welsh Terrier—easily distracted or intensely focused, which is, after all, how an earthdog must function. Take your eye off the target (be it rat, fox or badger) and you've lost the 'game'!

A similar scenario mistaken for obstinacy occurs when the dog is asked to obey a command that he has demonstrated over and over again that he can perform perfectly. Being a sensible dog, the Welsh Terrier sees nothing to be gained by pointless repetition.

The breed is intelligent and, as everyone knows, it isn't always easy to cope with intelligence. He is not a canine robot, but instead will show you (without having been asked) just how many different ways he can execute your request. It may be amusing to watch his mental wheels go round, and no harm is done so long as you remain amiably in control. The Welsh Terrier may have coined the phrase 'equal opportunity employer,' for he will seize every opportunity to become your equal, or better. If you drop your role as leader, rest assured your Welsh friend will retrieve it instantly. The Welsh Terrier is an intelligent, alert dog and great fun to teach basic obedience and home rules, even if a bit of a challenge.

TRAINABILITY
Begin as you mean to continue. Training begins from the moment the puppy (or adult) steps across the threshold of your household. Undeniably the best training method is bribery and coercion. Well, at least bribery! Later in this book, it is more politely referred to as 'positive reinforcement,' which means whenever the dog does as he's told, you hand out tiny food rewards. When he doesn't, you accept the fact that you did not properly explain what you wanted him to do, and you begin again. An occasional 'No!' is

All terriers are
curious, active
and easily
distracted—are
your family and
home ready for a
Welsh?

agreeing to be dressed up for
fantasy play. However, a Welsh
puppy is not a suitable new pet to
consider for a baby or for children
under the age of four or five years.
The puppy will treat these little
ones as littermates, and if you've
ever watched a litter of pups in
action, you know that needle-
sharp puppy teeth are invariably
involved in the play. Small
children who have never had a
puppy can't be expected to
understand.

Speaking of babies, it should
be pointed out that the Welsh
Terrier, regardless of age, is not a
baby and should never be treated
like one. He is a dog, knows he's a
dog and, what's more, is proud to
be one. He's also a terrier, which
makes him a bit more of a dog if
that's possible!

permissible, with an exaggerated
frown to signify your total
displeasure. Physical punishment
is definitely not acceptable and
might even encourage reciproca-
tion in kind. Welsh Terriers do
not have strong jaws and large
teeth for naught! It is wise not to
become involved in trading
smacks for bites.

House-training a Welsh Terrier
is seldom a problem when a
consistent schedule is followed,
ample praise is given for relieving
himself where he should, and the
dog is confined when no one is
free to keep an eye on him.

WITH YOUNGSTERS

A question often asked is how the
breed gets on with children. There
are two answers. The Welsh
Terrier is very good with slightly
older children; he is ready to obey
them and ready for almost any
game they want to play, even

THE BEST HOME

Given a choice, Welsh Terriers
would no doubt prefer to live in
the country, but will settle down
contentedly if a flat in the city is
where his family will be. In any
home with any type of garden or
outdoor area, a fence is essential
for the dog's safety in today's
world of motorways and busy
local traffic. The breed is not
given to excessive or senseless
barking, which is a blessing both
to owners and to neighbours, no
matter where you live.

The hunting instincts of the
breed make walks more than a

A well-behaved child and an equally well-behaved Welsh Terrier make a wonderful pair.

mere stroll down the lane. A brisk 30-minute walk with frequent stops for sniffing, exploring, tracking and greeting passers-by (human and canine) is ideal. Twice a day would be lovely. Once will suffice if augmented by vigorous games of fetch.

The Welsh Terrier is a calm housedog, not given to boisterous behaviour when adequately exercised. Most will alert you to a car or pedestrian coming up the path, but, to be honest, they are more apt to sound the alarm at an invasion by the neighbour's cat. Welsh Terriers raised with cats are generally tolerant of them, although one cannot always say the same for the cats! Introducing a cat into the home of an older Welsh unfamiliar with felines is another matter entirely. Proceed with a metric tonne of caution.

NOT QUITE PERFECT
As a Welsh Terrier owner, you may run into a behavioural problem based on something no one warned you about. It is called the Welsh Terrier Code of Ownership: 'What's mine is mine and if I have any part of it (or anything else) in my mouth, that's mine, too!' It's rather like dealing with a child in the 'terrible twos' stage! I don't mean to make light of it, however, for it can develop aggressive behaviour in an otherwise very compliant dog. It is not a game; you are dealing with a true terrier.

Never try to snatch anything away from the Welsh. You could be bitten in his attempt merely to hang onto his prize. Nor should you ever attempt to crawl under a bed or table to pull him out in order to retrieve your stockings. Not only will you meet those jaws again, but you are confronting an earthdog. When he retreats into a small dark place with something he caught (well, 'stole' is more accurate), he is in his totally natural element and will breach no mortal meddling in his domain.

The most you might achieve is a terrier battle of wits with the unpleasant sound of growling and the unacceptable appearance of curled lips and menacing teeth. The dog's owner needs to realise that he is actually causing the dog to react in this way. Let's say it's unacceptable behaviour on the part of the human.

How to avoid such confrontation? Easily, by the simple means of prevention. The day your Welsh Terrier enters your home, begin to teach 'drop it' or 'give it' by offering a tiny treat in your left hand while holding out your right hand to accept the surrendered toy. Food is always more desirable than a mere toy or even a stolen object. As with all training, gradually diminish the use of treats, but do keep up a verbal 'Good dog.' This clever trick could save the dog's life when he picks up a poisonous object (or makes off with your leather purse). Lure him out of hiding with a treat worth his while—a bit of cheese or sausage, for example.

Aggressive behaviour in any dog is dangerous. In the Welsh Terrier, as in any terrier, it is compounded by the dog's natural speed and the strength of its jaws. Luckily for us (and for the dogs), this turn of events is easily preventable in the normally good-natured Welsh Terrier.

Remember that Welsh Terriers are, above all, intelligent. They study and understand our body language more clearly than our words. Therefore, the exaggerated frown is a big help in relaying your message of disapproval. Welsh Terriers are also gluttons for treats and can be persuaded by food to do almost anything. If you ever hear a growl or a snarl, say 'No' with a big frown. Then quickly give the dog a familiar command, to which you can say 'Good dog' and give a reward. Gradually the food can be eliminated and verbal praise alone will be effective.

THE LASTING LOVE OF A WELSH

The Welsh Terrier is eager and able to take on whatever lifestyle is asked of him. He will be equally adept as a lap dog, foot warmer or companion to an elderly person, or, for the more active, as a hiking, hunting, swimming or boating chum. An interesting phenomenon about the Welsh Terrier is how faithful people are to the

DOGS, DOGS, GOOD FOR YOUR HEART!

People usually purchase dogs for companionship, but studies show that dogs can help to improve their owners' health and level of activity, as well as lower a human's risk of coronary heart disease. Without even realising it, when a person puts time into exercising, grooming and feeding a dog, he also puts more time into his own personal health care. Dog owners establish more routine schedules for their dogs to follow, which can have positive effects on a human's health. Dogs also teach us patience, offer unconditional love and provide the joy of having a furry friend to pet!

breed. Adults who grew up with Welsh Terriers invariably want the same breed for their children, and another when those children leave home and still another for their retirement years.

These small black and tan terriers have a unique way of fitting into each phase of our lives with charm, personality and sensible companionship that elicit an extreme loyalty in their owners. Airedale owners who, in their later years, can no longer cope with the size and strength of that breed, switch in great numbers to the Welsh. Then they often have to respond to that persistently annoying query, 'Is that a miniature Airedale?' with a somewhat defiant, 'No, sir (or madam). It is a Welsh Terrier!'

GOOD HEALTH

A genetically sound Welsh Terrier fed a good canine diet and given sufficient exercise and routine visits to the vet will live 12 to 15 years in good health. There are no health problems that are breed-specific, but those seen in all dogs, pure-bred and cross-bred, do occur now and then in the Welsh. Buying from a breeder with a good reputation for sound stock is the best way to avoid such genetic disorders as glaucoma, lens luxation, epilepsy or skin allergies.

There is no way to guarantee a lifetime free of all illness for any individual dog, but usually Welsh Terriers are an healthy, hardy lot. The explanation for this good fortune may lie in the fact that the breed has never become overly popular. Working with small numbers, dedicated breeders are quickly aware of any genetically transmitted disease and thus are able to remove affected animals from their breeding programmes.

ADDITIONAL ACCOMPLISHMENTS

While the reader has been taken through many of the charming ways in which a Welsh Terrier can usurp authority, it is not all a battle of wits. Here's a look at other uses for both his terrier tenacity and common sense.

THERAPY

As therapy dogs, Welsh Terriers are quite astonishing to behold. They quickly sense what is expected of them and become calm, almost serene, moving slowly and confidently among the ill and aged. They are unafraid of wheelchairs or

---

CORRECTIVE SURGERY

Surgery is often used to correct genetic bone diseases in dogs. Usually the problems present themselves early in the dog's life and must be treated before bone growth stops.

walkers, and are willing to be petted by unsteady hands.

AGILITY TRIALS
Agility must have been made for terriers! All those obstacles, jumps and tunnels are second nature to the Welsh Terrier's physical stamina, sense of adventure and his natural terrier instincts. To be realistic, however, getting him to cover the course in the required order is another matter entirely. Halfway through the tunnel, he may decide to wait for a fox to appear! However, do not despair. Keep your sense of humour and enjoy his amusing behaviour.

THE EARTHDOG
The reason these dogs were put on earth is—the *earth*! That is, to go to ground, and how they know it! Nothing can compare with the total body expression of a Welsh Terrier—eyes, ears, neck, tail— fired up by the smells of the earth, the natural hunting instinct put to the test. It makes little difference if the hunt is a natural one in the fields or along riverbanks, or in one of the artificial earths many countries use with protected fox, badger or vermin to test and maintain the working capabilities of the terriers. The Welsh Terrier is in his element and relishes the activity. Yet, on returning home, your friend will curl up near you by the fire, completely content.

Terrier means 'earth dog'...and any Welsh welcomes the opportunity to put his paws to work!

THE DELIGHTFUL DOG OF WALES
It's difficult to sum up these delightful Welsh dogs because they can be so diverse in personality and in the roles they play in our individual lives. I've tried to give you the bad along with the good, lest you think these black and tans belong on a pedestal. Indeed, they have their feet firmly on the ground with an heavenly, very high opinion of themselves.

It is useful to keep in mind that these dogs come from Wales, a country known for a folk tradition of argument or debate; perhaps the Welsh Terrier is carrying on that tradition. The dog is strong-willed (anything weaker would be no match for his natural prey), but with enough common sense to know when it is wiser to follow the rules. For that reason alone, the owner of a Welsh Terrier must be something of a Welsh Terrier himself, able to understand the debate but also able always to remain in charge.

Breed Standard for the
WELSH TERRIER

One initial obstacle for dog historians was the breeders' reluctance to use originality in naming their dogs. Literally hundreds of Welsh Terrier bitches named either Fan or Nell were further identified only occasionally by the owner's name. And how many Joneses would you guess there are in Wales? Since dogs changed owners from one show to the next, it was almost impossible to keep track of all the Fans and Nells. Major P F Brine took on the task of putting together a stud book for the Welsh Terrier Club with records going back to 1854. He completed this Herculean work in 1903.

Once founded, the Welsh Terrier Club (WTC) immediately set about drawing up a breed standard, which it completed in 1895. The first dog show breeders and judges were stockmen and horsemen whose great knowledge was based on the working aspects of their animals. 'Form follows function' was the rule and the reason why the original standard did not include the obvious. It remained unchanged until 1948,

when the breed height was raised from 15 to 15.5 inches, a decision arrived at jointly by the WTC and the Welsh Terrier Association (WTA). The new format in which the standard appears today was approved by The Kennel Club in 1994.

The Kennel Club standard was used in the US until 1984,

THE IDEAL SPECIMEN

According to The Kennel Club, 'The Breed Standard is the "Blueprint" of the ideal specimen in each breed approved by a governing body, e.g. The Kennel Club, the Fédération Cynologique Internationale (FCI) and the American Kennel Club.

'The Kennel Club writes and revises Breed Standards taking account of the advice of Breed Councils/Clubs. Breed Standards are not changed lightly to avoid "changing the standard to fit the current dogs" and the health and well-being of future dogs is always taken into account when new standards are prepared or existing ones altered.'

when parts of it were re-written in an effort to translate it into 'American English.' To assist new breeders unfamiliar with breed vernacular, the Welsh Terrier Club of America publishes an annotated standard, 'The Welsh Terrier in Profile,' which explains in detail and with sketches each portion of the standard.

The standard is a blueprint or written description of the perfect dog, and thus serves to train the breeder's eye. It serves as a quick reference sheet for the show judge. Although one cannot quarrel with obvious deviations from it, nevertheless every breed standard is open to subjective interpretation. One person may wish to forgive a slightly gay tail and focus instead on the lovely head, while another observer sees that gay tail as a major defect, taking precedence over the nice head.

In judging the Welsh Terrier, whether by qualified conformation judges, breeders or ringside spectators, the emphasis must be on the working aspect of the dog and thus on soundness, not mere beauty. A dog with a weak front or hindquarters, or one with too short a back, or with a quarrelsome temperament, could not perform a productive day's work.

The lovely alert eye and ear expression of a Welsh Terrier, combined with good ears and set-on of tail, are the beauty aspects of the dog, referred to as 'type.' Soundness and type must be considered jointly to be judged against that unattainable perfect specimen as described in the standard.

Mr Walter Glynn's description is as valid today as when he wrote it one-hundred years ago: 'The Welsh Terrier is built on the lines of a powerful, short-legged, short-backed hunter. He is best with a jet black back and neck, and deep tan head, ears, legs and tail; ears a shade deeper than elsewhere.' You will note that soundness is foremost.

The most notable change in the Welsh Terrier seen from pictures of the early show dogs to those of the present is the acquisition of face and leg furnishings (the profusion of fuzzy hair on those parts). Since no farmer or miner of the day would have bothered to pluck out the hair in these areas, it is apparent that the breed originally had little or no excess hair on their legs or muzzles. The furnishings came about with the beauty aspect of the dog shows. It wasn't until the late 1920s and '30s that these were considered essential parts of the Welsh Terrier's show coat. As professional handlers in America became accomplished canine cosmetologists, more emphasis was placed on growing any hair that could then be trimmed and shaped to fool an unwary judge.

A male Welsh Terrier of correct type and balance.

In Britain and on the Continent, the Welsh Terrier is shown in a somewhat more natural, or workmanlike, state than in America.

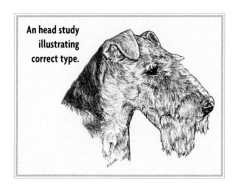

An head study illustrating correct type.

THE KENNEL CLUB BREED STANDARD FOR THE WELSH TERRIER

General Appearance: Smart, workmanlike, well balanced and compact.

Characteristics: Affectionate, obedient and easily controlled.

Temperament: Happy and volatile, rarely of shy nature. Game and fearless but definitely not aggressive although at times able to hold his own when necessary.

Head and Skull: Flat, of moderate width between ears. Jaws powerful, clean cut, rather deep and punishing. Stop not too defined, medium length from stop to end of nose. Nose black.

Eyes: Small, well set in, dark, expression indicative of temperament. A round, full eye desirable.

Ears: V-shaped, small, leathers not too thin, set on fairly high, carried forward and close to cheek.

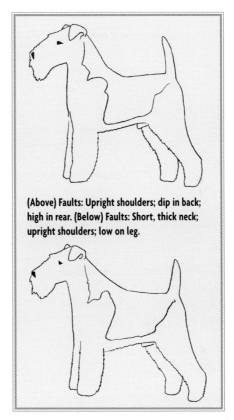

(Above) Faults: Upright shoulders; dip in back; high in rear. (Below) Faults: Short, thick neck; upright shoulders; low on leg.

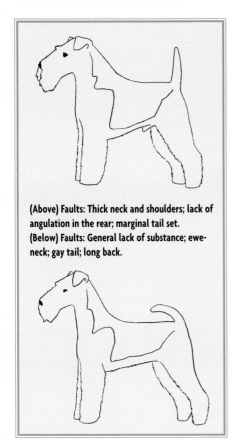

(Above) Faults: Thick neck and shoulders; lack of angulation in the rear; marginal tail set. (Below) Faults: General lack of substance; ewe-neck; gay tail; long back.

Mouth: Jaws strong with perfect, regular scissor bite, i.e. upper teeth closely overlapping lower teeth and set square to the jaws.

Neck: Moderate length and thickness, slightly arched and sloping gracefully into shoulders.

Forequarters: Shoulders long, sloping and well set back. Legs straight and muscular, possessing ample bone, with upright and powerful pasterns.

Comparing type in the Welsh (left) and Wire-haired Fox Terrier (right). The Welsh is stockier, with more substance. The Fox Terrier has a longer, narrower head, with smaller, high-set ears.

Body: Back short and well ribbed up, loin strong, good depth and moderate width of chest.

Hindquarters: Strong, thighs muscular, of good length, with hocks well bent, well let down and with ample bone.

Feet: Small, round and cat-like.

Tail: Well set on but not carried too gaily. Customarily docked.

Gait/Movement: Fore- and hindlegs carried straight forward and parallel. Elbows move perpendicular to body, working free of sides, stifles turning neither in nor out.

Coat: Wiry, hard, very close and abundant. Single coat undesirable.

Colour: Black and tan for preference, or black grizzle and tan, free from black pencilling on toes. Black below hocks most undesirable.

Size: Height at shoulder not exceeding 39 cms (15.5 ins). Weight: 9–9.5 kgs (20–21 lbs).

Faults: Any departure from the foregoing points should be considered a fault and the seriousness with which the fault should be regarded should be in exact proportion to its degree.

Note: Male animals should have two apparently normal testicles fully descended into the scrotum.

BREEDER'S BLUEPRINT

If you are considering breeding your bitch, it is very important that you are familiar with the breed standard. Reputable breeders breed with the intention of producing dogs that are as close as possible to the standard and that contribute to the advancement of the breed. Study the standard for both physical appearance and temperament, and make certain your bitch and your chosen stud dog measure up.

Welsh Terriers in conformation showing are not compared against one another; rather, they are compared to the breed standard to determine which one's attributes most closely resemble those of the ideal dog.

Proven quality in a champion: Fin & Est Ch Vicway Live Free or Die, owned by Mr Juha Korhonen, was World Winner in 1998.

PUPPY APPEARANCE

Your puppy should have a well-fed appearance but not a distended abdomen, which may indicate worms or incorrect feeding, or both. The body should be firm, with a solid feel. The skin of the abdomen should be pale pink and clean, without signs of scratching or rash. Check the hind legs to make certain that dewclaws were removed, if any were present at birth.

SELECTING A PUPPY

You'll notice a few things when taking your first look at a Welsh litter. If you see the Welsh pups at three or four weeks of age, they are apt to be almost entirely black. However, the tan increases in all the right places as the pups mature. Also, don't worry if the dam is a bit protective of her brood; that's normal.

Nine to ten weeks is the ideal age to bring a Welsh puppy into your life. Each puppy needs that much time to learn that he is a dog, how to behave as a dog and—so very importantly—how to read the body language of other dogs. A misunderstanding in the latter is usually the spark that sets off a fight. The Welsh can best learn all of this from his dam and littermates. The physical, and sometimes vocal, activity among littermates is part of the essential learning experience.

Unless you have previously owned a Welsh Terrier, know something about the breed and consider yourself to be a 'terrier person,' I would not advise you to select the most active pup in the litter. In some breeds, that would be exactly the pup to choose, but not in the Welsh Terrier. The one

PUPPY SELECTION

Your selection of a good puppy can be determined by your needs. A show potential or a good pet? It is your choice. Every puppy, however, should be of good temperament. Although show-quality puppies are bred and raised with emphasis on physical conformation, responsible breeders strive for equally good temperament. Do not buy from a breeder who concentrates solely on physical beauty at the expense of personality.

best!' That one may be destined for the show ring, or could be a nice pet with a good attitude. A calm, somewhat quiet puppy may be sizing you up as a potential partner. At the other end of the temperament scale is the shy pup. True shyness is almost unheard of

Bring the family along when visiting the litter. Everyone should take part in selecting the new puppy.

that wants to continue to play energetically when the others stop is not going to be an easy pup to convince that he must take his orders from you! He will need a pleasant but very firm, very consistent hand to tone down his natural exuberance, which otherwise will become dominance.

There is also the pup that looks you straight in the eye with a look that says, 'See me? I'm the

DID YOU KNOW?

You should not even think about buying a puppy that looks sick, undernourished, overly frightened or nervous. Sometimes a timid puppy will warm up to you after a 30-minute 'let's-get-acquainted' session.

in Welsh Terriers, so beware the pup that shuns your hand or creeps away to sit by himself. That one may require the help of a professional behaviourist before too long.

Choose any one of the happy,

YOUR SCHEDULE . . .
If you lead an erratic, unpredictable life, with daily or weekly changes in your work requirements, consider the problems of owning a puppy. The new puppy has to be fed regularly, socialised (loved, petted, handled, introduced to other people) and, most importantly, allowed to visit outdoors for toilet training. As the dog gets older, it can be more tolerant of deviations in its feeding and toilet relief.

friendly, normal Welsh pups wanting to kiss your hands, nibble your fingers or just have your attention. The chances are good that you won't even be confronted with either of the two extremes.

PUPPY NEEDS AND DEVELOPMENT

Your Welsh Terrier puppy will need all-day everyday attention for about six weeks. The routine of feeding, house-training and exercise is broken only by frequent naps (yours coinciding with the pup's). If you are not there to teach the puppy what he can do (as well as where and when) and what he cannot ever do, he will instantly teach himself. If he gets away with something naughty because no one was there to tell him otherwise, the puppy will have taught himself that it was the right thing to do. And he'll do it again. The owner is the teacher, guidance counsellor and correction official.

At any time between five and seven months, a Welsh Terrier may go through what is commonly called a fear phase, when the normally outgoing, happy pup may suddenly seem shy or fearful. The phase can last a day or a few weeks and the best way to live through it is not to give in to it. Keep the pup with you (on lead, if necessary) and go about your business using a

PREPARING FOR PUP

Unfortunately, when a puppy is bought by someone who does not take into consideration the time and attention that dog ownership requires, it is the puppy who suffers when he is either abandoned or placed in a shelter by a frustrated owner. So all of the 'homework' you do in preparation for your pup's arrival will benefit you both. The more informed you are, the more you will know what to expect and the better equipped you will be to handle the ups and downs of raising a puppy. Hopefully, everyone in the household is willing to do his part in raising and caring for the pup. The anticipation of owning a dog often brings a lot of promises from excited family members: 'I will walk him every day,' 'I will feed him,' 'I will house-train him,' etc., but these things take time and effort, and promises can easily be forgotten once the novelty of the new pet has worn off.

'It's all okay' because it most decidedly is not so in the pup's mind. Use the cheerful chat distraction routine, add some toys and turn up the TV.

After giving you all that advice, however, the vast majority of Welsh Terriers do not go through this phase for more than five minutes. It may be due to their conviction that they will all grow up to be Airedales! Although the Welsh reaches full height by ten months of age, he is not fully mature and in fact will probably begin a period of teenage nonsense. By the age of two years, he will be a self-confident adult.

INDOOR/OUTDOOR

A Welsh Terrier is not a dog to be left outdoors despite his harsh coat and hardy physique. He thrives on social interaction with

normal tone of voice and lots of cheerful chat. Ask your guests to pay no attention until the pup makes the first overture. All this is Nature's way of cautioning the rapidly maturing puppy to slow down. Fear of thunderstorms is quite different. That is Nature's way of telling all animals to seek shelter. Don't fall into the trap of cuddling your puppy and saying

Outdoors on a rainy day is no place for the family dog. Your Welsh is a rugged outdoorsman, but he thrives on the companionship of his family and the comforts of home.

INSURANCE
Many good breeders will offer you insurance with your new puppy, which is an excellent idea. The first few weeks of insurance will probably be covered free of charge or with only minimal cost, allowing you to take up the policy when this expires. If you own a pet dog, it is sensible to take out such a policy as veterinary fees can be high, although routine vaccinations and boosters are not covered. Look carefully at the many options open to you before deciding which suits you best.

his family and craves the creature comforts of his home. If you don't want a dog to 'help' make the tea or the beds, rearrange the flowers or read a book tucked up close to you, forget the Welsh. He won't be underfoot, just close by because he is certain you'll need his assistance any minute.

IF YOU'D PREFER AN ADULT
If you do not have the time needed to teach a puppy all he must learn, there are several ways to obtain an adult Welsh Terrier. Breeders often have a dog or bitch that has finished its show or breeding career—or perhaps never lived up to its potential. There are also dogs in need of adoption for any number of reasons, such as the death of a previous owner or an irresponsible, impulsive

DID YOU KNOW?
Breeders rarely release puppies until they are nine to ten weeks of age. This is an acceptable age for most breeds of dog, excepting toy breeds, which are not released until around 12 weeks, given their petite sizes. If a breeder has a puppy that is 12 weeks of age or older, it is likely well socialised and house-trained. Be sure that it is otherwise healthy before deciding to take it home.

ARE YOU A FIT OWNER?

If the breeder from whom you are buying a Welsh Terrier asks you a lot of personal questions, do not be insulted. Such a breeder wants to be sure that you will be a fit provider for his dog, puppy or adult.

owner's abandonment. Contact the Welsh Terrier club nearest you and follow their advice.

The only caveat is that the adult was trained, rightly or wrongly, by someone else. The adult Welsh coming into a new home will have all the basic things to learn, such as your house rules, the family members, your home routine, the words you use, the sounds, smells and sights. He will also have an equal amount to un-learn, including habits that you may not permit in your home. Welsh Terriers are not one-man dogs, although they are skilled at making each of their owners think otherwise. There will be an adjustment period and at some point the dog may indicate that it has been pleasant visiting with you, but now he'd like to go home. On the other hand, he may think he's landed in Heaven and never look back. Either way, as soon as he settles in, the new owner will become his best friend. As I've said, the Welsh Terrier is a very sensible dog.

DOG OR BITCH?

The prevalent view is that all males are aggressive watchdogs and all bitches will be sweet, stay close to home and look after the children. This is pure rubbish! The differences in Welsh Terrier temperament and character are

DOCUMENTATION

Two important documents you will get from the breeder are the pup's pedigree and registration certificate. The breeder should register the litter and each pup with The Kennel Club, and it is necessary for you to have the paperwork if you plan on showing or breeding in the future.

Make sure you know the breeder's intentions on which type of registration he will obtain for the pup. There are limited registrations which may prohibit the dog from being shown, bred or competing in non-conformation trials such as Working or Agility if the breeder feels that the pup is not of sufficient quality to do so. There is also a type of registration that will permit the dog in non-conformation competition only.

On the reverse side of the registration certificate, the new owner can find the transfer section, which must be signed by the breeder.

almost non-existent. Males are slightly larger and, properly raised, are complete gentlemen. Bitches can be very sweet and feminine—or not. Go with the individual pup you are attracted to and, in either case, have it neutered by six months of age. It is a fallacy that such surgery will keep either sex closer to home, or make it fat or lazy. It will restrain the hormones, however.

Like most of the other terriers, the Welsh Terriers do best with terrier-like people. These are people who are themselves alert, ready to go and inquisitive, but calm, self-assured and sensible. This is not the breed for the meek and mild or indecisive.

BOY OR GIRL?
While in many breeds, gender differences may play a big role in one's selection of a puppy, this is not the case with the Welsh Terrier. Differences between the male and female Welsh are minimal, and the mutual attraction between you and the individual pup should be the most important factor in your decision. For a pet dog that is not destined for breeding or the show ring, neutering the male or spaying the female is important, as it reduces the risk of certain health problems and may guarantee your pet a longer life.

Visiting the breeder's facilities says a lot about the breeder and how he cares for his dogs. View the litter, meet the other dogs on the premises, see where the dogs are kept and exercised, etc.

COMMITMENT OF OWNERSHIP
After considering all of these factors, you have most likely already made some very important decisions about selecting your puppy. You have chosen a Welsh Terrier, which means that you have decided which characteristics you want in a dog and what type of dog will best fit into your family and lifestyle. If you have selected a breeder, you have gone a step further—you have done your research and found a responsible, conscientious person who breeds quality Welsh Terriers and who should be a reliable source of help as you and your puppy adjust to life together. If you have observed a litter in action, you have obtained a firsthand look at the dynamics of a puppy 'pack' and,

thus, you have learned about each pup's individual personality—perhaps you have even found one that particularly appeals to you.

However, even if you have not yet found the Welsh Terrier puppy of your dreams, observing pups will help you learn to recognise certain behaviour and to determine what a pup's behaviour indicates about his temperament. You will be able to pick out which pups are the leaders, which ones are less outgoing, which ones are confident, which ones are shy, playful, friendly, aggressive, etc. Equally as important, you will learn to recognise what an healthy pup should look and act like. All of these things will help you in your search, and when you find the Welsh Terrier that was meant for you, you will know it!

Researching your breed, selecting a responsible breeder and

FEEDING TIPS
You will probably start feeding your pup the same food that he has been getting from the breeder; the breeder should give you a few days' supply to start you off. Although you should not give your pup too many treats, you will want to have puppy treats on hand for coaxing, training, rewards, etc. Be careful, though, as a small pup's calorie requirements are relatively low and a few treats can add up to almost a full day's worth of calories without the required nutrition.

HANDLE WITH CARE
You should be extremely careful about handling tiny puppies. Not that you might hurt them, but that the pups' mother may exhibit what is called 'maternal aggression.' It is a natural, instinctive reaction for the dam to protect her young against anything she interprets as predatory or possibly harmful to her pups.

The sweetest, most gentle of bitches, after whelping a litter, often react this way even to her owner.

observing as many pups as possible are all important steps on the way to dog ownership. It may seem like a lot of effort...and you have not even taken the pup home yet! Remember, though, you cannot be too careful when it comes to deciding on the type of dog you want and finding out about your prospective pup's background. Buying a puppy is not—or should not be—just another whimsical purchase. This is one instance in which you actually do get to choose your own family! You may be thinking that buying a puppy should be fun—it should not be so serious and so much work. Keep in mind that your puppy is not a cuddly stuffed toy or decorative lawn ornament; rather, he is a living creature that will become a real member of your family. You will come to realise that, while buying a puppy is a pleasurable and exciting endeavour, it is not something to be taken lightly. Relax...the fun will start when the pup comes home!

Always keep in mind that a puppy is nothing more than a baby in a furry disguise...a baby who is virtually helpless in a human world and who trusts his owner for fulfilment of his basic needs for survival. In addition to food, water and shelter, your pup needs care, protection, guidance and love. If you are not prepared to commit to this, then you are not prepared to own a dog.

Wait a minute, you say. How hard could this be? All of my neighbours own dogs and they seem to be doing just fine. Why should I have to worry about all of this? Well, you should not worry about it; in fact, you will probably find that once your Welsh Terrier pup gets used to his new home, he will fall into his

> **QUALITY FOOD**
> The cost of food must be mentioned. All dogs need a good-quality food with an adequate supply of protein to develop their bones and muscles properly. Most dogs are not picky eaters but, unless fed properly, can quickly succumb to skin problems.

place in the family quite naturally. However, it never hurts to emphasise the commitment of dog ownership. With some time and patience, it is really not too difficult to raise a curious and exuberant Welsh Terrier pup to be a well-adjusted and well-mannered adult dog—a dog that could be your most loyal friend.

PREPARING PUPPY'S PLACE IN YOUR HOME
Researching your breed and finding a breeder are only two aspects of the 'homework' you will have to do before taking your Welsh Terrier puppy home. You will also have to prepare your home and family for the new addition. Much as you would prepare a nursery for a newborn baby, you will need to designate a place in your home that will be the puppy's own. How you prepare your home will depend on how much freedom the dog will be allowed. Whatever you decide, you must ensure that he

has a place that he can 'call his own.'

When you bring your new puppy into your home, you are bringing him into what will become his home as well. Obviously, you did not buy a puppy with the intentions of catering to his every whim and allowing him to 'rule the roost,' but in order for a puppy to grow into a stable, well-adjusted dog, he has to feel comfortable in his surroundings. Remember, he is leaving the warmth and security of his mother and littermates, as well as the familiarity of the only place he has ever known, so it is important to make his transition as easy as possible. By preparing a place in your home for the puppy, you are making him feel as welcome as possible in a strange new place. It should not take him long to get used to it, but the sudden shock of being trans-planted is somewhat traumatic for a young pup. Imagine how a small child would feel in the same situation—that is how your puppy must be feeling. It is up to you to reassure him and to let him know, 'Little chap, you are going to like it here!'

WHAT YOU SHOULD BUY

CRATE
To someone unfamiliar with the use of crates in dog training, it may seem like punishment to shut a dog in a crate, but this is not the case at all. Although all breeders do not advocate crate training, more and more breeders and trainers are recommending crates as preferred tools for show puppies as well as pet puppies.

Crates are not cruel—crates have many humane and highly effective uses in dog care and training. For example, crate training is a popular and successful house-training method.

Your local pet shop will have a selection of crates from which you may choose one that best suits your needs.

PHOTO COURTESY OF DOSKOCIL

In addition, a crate can keep your dog safe during travel and, perhaps most importantly, a crate provides your dog with a place of his own in your home. It serves as a 'doggie bedroom' of sorts—your Welsh Terrier can curl up in his crate when he wants to sleep or when he just needs a break. Many dogs sleep in their crates overnight. With soft bedding and his favourite toy, a crate becomes a cosy pseudo-den for your dog. Like his ancestors, he too will seek out the comfort and retreat of a den—you just happen to be providing him with something a little more luxurious than what his early ancestors enjoyed.

As far as purchasing a crate, the type that you buy is up to you. It will most likely be one of the two most popular types: wire or fibreglass. There are advantages and disadvantages to each type. For example, a wire crate is more open, allowing the air to flow

In addition to a crate, your Welsh will appreciate a cosy dog bed. Be aware, though, that a wicker basket can be destroyed in short order by a chewing pup.

CRATE TRAINING TIPS

During crate training, you should partition off the section of the crate in which the pup stays. If he is given too big an area, this will hinder your training efforts. Crate training is based on the fact that a dog does not like to soil his sleeping quarters, so it is ineffective to keep a pup in a crate that is so big that he can eliminate in one end and get far enough away from it to sleep. Also, you want to make the crate den-like for the pup. Blankets and a favourite toy will make the crate cosy for the small pup; as he grows, you may want to evict some of his 'roommates' to make more room.

It will take some coaxing at first, but be patient. Given some time to get used to it, your pup will adapt to his new home-within-a-home quite nicely.

through and affording the dog a view of what is going on around him, while a fibreglass crate is sturdier. Both can double as travel crates, providing protection for the dog. The size of the crate is another thing to consider. Puppies do not stay puppies forever—in fact, sometimes it seems as if they grow right before your eyes. A very small crate may be fine for a very young Welsh Terrier pup, but it will not do him much good for long! Unless you have the money and the inclination to buy a new crate every time your pup has a

growth spurt, it is better to get one that will accommodate your dog both as a pup and at full size.

The size of the crate is another thing to consider, but for the Welsh Terrier you will only need to do so once. A crate approximately 56 cms (22 ins) long by 46 cms (18 ins) wide by 49 cms (19 ins) high will last the Welsh's lifetime.

The crate begins as his special puppy place to be, and as his bed overnight with the door closed. With the door left open during the day, the crate is his den where he can put his toys and be by himself for a nap. A special feature of the crate is the travel aspect, not just for safety in the car, but when you go off visiting friends and relatives, the crate is the dog's home away from home, making him feel 'at home' even when he's not. The crate is the 'den' of the earthdog.

BEDDING

Veterinary bedding in the dog's crate will help the dog feel more at home, and you may also like to pop in a small blanket. First, this will take the place of the leaves, twigs, etc., that the pup would use in the wild to make a den; the pup can make his own 'burrow' in the crate. Although your pup is far removed from his den-making ancestors, the denning instinct is still a part of his genetic makeup. Second, until you take your pup

TEETHING TIP
Puppies like soft toys for chewing. Because they are teething, soft items like stuffed toys soothe their aching gums, but always monitor pups when they are playing with potentially destructible toys.

home, he has been sleeping amid the warmth of his mother and littermates, and while a blanket is not the same as a warm, breathing body, it still provides heat and something with which to snuggle. You will want to wash your pup's bedding frequently in case he has a toileting 'accident' in his crate, and replace or remove any blanket that becomes ragged and starts to fall apart.

TOYS

Plush squeaky toys are the earthdogs' favourites! What else is there that is soft and squashy and squeals like a cornered rat? All

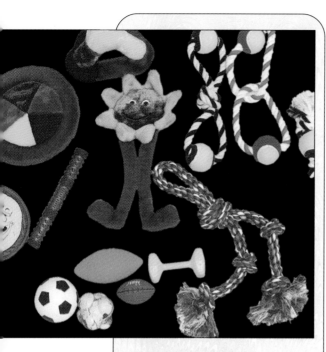

From the wide array of leads available, choose a durable yet lightweight lead for your Welsh Terrier.

TOYS, TOYS, TOYS!

With a big variety of dog toys available, and so many that look like they would be a lot of fun for a dog, be careful in your selection. It is amazing what a set of puppy teeth can do to an innocent-looking toy, so, obviously, safety is a major consideration. Be sure to choose the most durable products that you can find. Hard nylon bones and toys are a safe bet, and many of them are offered in different scents and flavours that will be sure to capture your dog's attention. It is always fun to play a game of catch with your dog, and there are balls and flying discs that are specially made to withstand dog teeth.

Welsh puppies enjoy them. Indulge your pup, but monitor all toys and get rid of any that have been chewed to divulge the stuffing or squeaker. Some Welsh Terriers will play with a squeaky toy for years, even after it no longer squeaks. Admittedly, others will destroy the entire toy in half an hour. If your dog is one of the latter, you'll have to forego the squeaky variety and stick with heavy-duty rubber or knotted rope toys and large knucklebones.

You can make an excellent puppy teething toy out of a knotted piece of towel, dampened and put in the fridge for an hour or so. Chewing into the cold towelling relieves itchy gums caused by the new teeth's erupting and provides good exercise for the jaws. An inexpensive, beneficial toy!

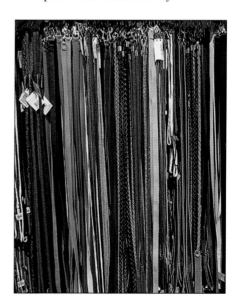

LEAD

A nylon lead is probably the best option, as it is the most resistant to puppy teeth should your pup take a liking to chewing on his lead. Of course, this is a habit that should be nipped in the bud, but, if your pup likes to chew on his lead, he has a very slim chance of being able to chew through the strong nylon. Nylon leads are also lightweight, which is good for a young Welsh Terrier who is just getting used to the idea of walking on a lead. For everyday walking and safety purposes, the nylon lead is a good choice. As your pup grows up and gets used to walking on the lead, you may want to purchase a flexible lead. These leads allow you to extend the length to give the dog a

This Welsh pup is becoming accustomed to his nylon lead, attached to a sturdy, light collar.

broader area to explore or to shorten the length to keep the dog near you.

The best lead for training is a 2-metre (6-foot) cotton lead. It is gentle on your hands and won't slip as easily as nylon. Welsh Terriers are generally co-operative about this 'attachment for safety' programme of ours. As an adult, when he won't be so apt to chew it to bits, your Welsh Terrier will look quite handsome with a matching leather collar and lead.

COLLAR

Your pup should get used to wearing a collar all the time since you will want to attach his ID tags to it; plus, you have to attach the lead to something! A lightweight nylon collar is a good choice. Make certain that the collar fits snugly enough so that the pup cannot wriggle out of it, but is loose enough so that it will not be uncomfortably tight around the pup's neck.

FINANCIAL RESPONSIBILITY

Grooming tools, collars, leashes, dog beds and, of course, toys will be an expense to you when you first obtain your pup, and the cost will continue throughout your dog's lifetime. If your puppy damages or destroys your possessions (as most puppies surely will!) or something belonging to a neighbour, you can calculate additional expense. There is also flea and pest control, which every dog owner faces more than once. You must be able to handle the financial responsibility of owning a dog.

CHOOSE AN APPROPRIATE COLLAR

The **BUCKLE COLLAR** is the standard collar used for everyday purposes. Be sure that you adjust the buckle on growing puppies. Check it every day. It can become too tight overnight! These collars can be made of leather or nylon. Attach your dog's identification tags to this collar.

The **CHOKE COLLAR** is constructed of highly polished steel so that it slides easily through the stainless steel loop. The idea is that the dog controls the pressure around its neck and he will stop pulling if the collar becomes uncomfortable. It should *not* be used on the Welsh Terrier.

The **HALTER** is for a trained dog that has to be restrained to prevent running away, chasing a cat and the like. Considered the most humane of all collars, it is frequently used on smaller dogs for which collars are not comfortable.

Welsh puppies seldom object to any collar for more than a few minutes. The martingale collar (which is a double loop) prevents the dog from backing out as well as allowing you to make gentle corrections when he lunges ahead. It can be used for training as well. For the more athletic types, or those Welsh Terriers resistant to class instruction, an Halti head collar is the answer. The Halti is an attention-getting device that allows you to turn the dog's head toward you, giving you better control over those persistent terrier distractions. Choke collars should never be used; the Halti is more conducive to mutual understanding.

FOOD AND WATER BOWLS

Your pup will need two bowls, one for food and one for water. You may want two sets of bowls, one for indoors and one for outdoors, depending on where the dog will be fed and where he will be spending time. Stainless steel or sturdy plastic bowls are popular choices. Plastic bowls are more chewable, but dogs tend not to chew on the steel variety, which can be sterilised. It is important to buy sturdy bowls since anything is in danger of being chewed by puppy teeth and you do not want your dog to be constantly chewing apart his bowl (for his safety and for your purse!).

Choose sturdy food and water bowls, in suitable sizes, for your Welsh Terrier.

PHOTO COURTESY OF MIKKI PET PRODUCTS.

It is your respon-
sibility to clean
up after your
Welsh Terrier has
relieved itself. Pet
shops have
various aids to
assist in the
clean-up task.

CLEANING SUPPLIES

Until a pup is house-trained, you
will be doing a lot of cleaning.
'Accidents' will occur, which is
acceptable in the beginning stages
of toilet training because the
puppy does not know any better.
All you can do is be prepared to
clean up any accidents as soon as
they happen. Old rags, towels,
newspapers and a safe disinfec-
tant are good to have on hand.

BEYOND THE BASICS

The items previously discussed
are the bare necessities. You will
find out what else you need as
you go along—grooming supplies,
flea/tick protection, baby gates to
partition a room, etc. These things
will vary depending on your
situation, but it is important that

you have everything you need to
feed and make your Welsh Terrier
comfortable in his first few days at
home.

PUPPY-PROOFING YOUR HOME

Aside from making sure that your
Welsh Terrier will be comfortable
in your home, you also have to
make sure that your home is safe
for your Welsh Terrier. This
means taking precautions that
your pup will not get into
anything he should not get into
and that there is nothing within
his reach that may harm him
should he sniff it, chew it, inspect
it, etc. This probably seems
obvious since, while you are
primarily concerned with your
pup's safety, at the same time you
do not want your belongings to be
ruined. Breakables should be
placed out of reach if your dog is
to have full run of the house. If he
is to be limited to certain places
within the house, keep any
potentially dangerous items in the
'off-limits' areas.

An electrical cord can pose a
danger should the puppy decide
to taste it—and who is going to
convince a pup that it would not
make a great chew toy? Cords
should be fastened tightly against
the wall. If your dog is going to
spend time in a crate, make sure
that there is nothing near his crate
that he can reach if he sticks his
curious little nose or paws
through the openings. Just as you

TOXIC PLANTS

Many plants can be toxic to dogs. If you see your dog carrying a piece of vegetation in his mouth, approach him in a quiet, disinterested manner, avoid eye contact, pet him and gradually remove the plant from his mouth. Alternatively, offer him a treat and maybe he'll drop the plant on his own accord. Be sure no toxic plants are growing in your own garden.

would with a child, keep all household cleaners and chemicals where the pup cannot reach them.

It is also important to make sure that the outside of your home is safe. Of course, your puppy should never be unsupervised, but a pup let loose in the garden will want to run and explore, and he should be granted that freedom. Do not let a fence give you a false sense of security; you would be surprised at how crafty (and persistent) a dog can be in working out how to dig under and squeeze his way through small holes, or to jump or climb over a fence. The remedy is to make the fence well embedded into the ground and high enough so that it really is impossible for your dog to get over it (about 3 metres should suffice).

Be sure to repair or secure any gaps in the fence. Check the fence periodically to ensure that it is in good shape and make repairs as

needed; a very determined pup may return to the same spot to 'work on it' until he is able to get through. Be very careful about doors that open into unfenced areas. Each family member must be on guard lest the Welsh Terrier slip out unnoticed.

FIRST TRIP TO THE VET

You have selected your puppy, and your home and family are ready. Now all you have to do is collect your Welsh Terrier from the breeder and the fun begins, right? Well...not so fast. Something else you need to plan is your pup's first trip to the veterinary surgeon. Perhaps the breeder can recommend someone in the area who specialises in terriers, or maybe you know some other Welsh Terrier owners who can suggest a good vet. Either

Your Welsh Terrier puppy will be very curious about his new home and surroundings. Be sure that the garden is securely enclosed, and that there are no dangerous plants or toxic chemicals in your landscaping.

way, you should have an appoint-
ment arranged for your pup before
you pick him up.

The pup's first visit will
consist of an overall examination
to make sure that the pup does
not have any problems that are
not apparent to you. The veterinary surgeon will also set up a
schedule for the pup's
vaccinations; the breeder will
inform you of which ones the pup
has already received and the vet
can continue from there.

INTRODUCTION TO THE FAMILY

Everyone in the house will be
excited about the puppy's coming
home and will want to pet him
and play with him, but it is best
to make the introduction low-key
so as not to overwhelm the puppy.
He is apprehensive already. It is
the first time he has been
separated from his mother and the
breeder, and the ride to your
home is likely to be the first time
he has been in a car. The last
thing you want to do is smother
him, as this will only frighten him
further. This is not to say that
human contact is not extremely
necessary at this stage, because
this is the time when a connection
between the pup and his human
family is formed. Gentle petting
and soothing words should help
console him, as well as just
putting him down and letting him
explore on his own (under your

> **HOW VACCINES WORK**
> If you've just bought a puppy, you
> surely know the importance of
> having your pup vaccinated, but do
> you understand how vaccines work?
> Vaccines contain the same bacteria
> or viruses that cause the disease
> you want to prevent, but they have
> been chemically modified so that
> they don't cause any harm. Instead,
> the vaccine causes your dog to
> produce antibodies that fight the
> harmful bacteria. Thus, if your pup
> is exposed to the disease in the
> future, the antibodies will destroy
> the viruses or bacteria.

watchful eye, of course).

The pup may approach the
family members or may busy
himself with exploring for a
while. Gradually, each person
should spend some time with the
pup, one at a time, crouching
down to get as close to the pup's
level as possible, letting him sniff
their hands and petting him
gently. He definitely needs human
attention and he needs to be
touched—this is how to form an
immediate bond. Just remember
that the pup is experiencing many
things for the first time, at the
same time. There are new people,
new noises, new smells and new
things to investigate, so be gentle,
be affectionate and be as
comforting as you can be.

PUP'S FIRST NIGHT HOME

You have travelled home with your new charge safely in his crate. He's been to the vet for a thorough check-up; he's been weighed, his papers have been examined and perhaps he's even been vaccinated and wormed as well. He's met (and licked!) the whole family, including the excited children and the less-than-happy cat. He's explored his area, his new bed, the garden and anywhere else he's been permitted. He's eaten his first meal at home and relieved himself in the proper place. He's heard lots of new sounds, smelled new friends and seen more of the outside world than ever before... and that was just the first day!

He's worn out and is ready for bed...or so you think!

It's puppy's first night home and you are ready to say 'Good night.' Keep in mind that this is his first night ever to be sleeping alone. His dam and littermates are no longer at paw's length and he's a bit scared, cold and lonely. Be reassuring to your new family member, but this is not the time to spoil him and give in to his inevitable whining.

Puppies whine. They whine to let others know where they are and hopefully to get company out of it. Place your pup in his new bed or crate in his designated area and close the door. Mercifully, he may fall asleep without a peep. When the inevitable occurs,

Consider your pup's safety both indoors and out, by puppy-proofing and supervising. A pup doesn't know the difference between an electrical cord and a chew toy, which could lead to danger.

however, ignore the whining—he is fine. Be strong and keep his interest in mind. Do not allow yourself to feel guilty and visit the pup. He will fall asleep eventually.

Many breeders recommend placing a piece of bedding from the pup's former home in his new bed so that he recognises and is comforted by the scent of his littermates. Others still advise placing a hot water bottle in the bed for warmth. The latter may be a good idea provided the pup doesn't attempt to suckle—he'll get good and wet, and may not fall asleep so fast.

Puppy's first night can be somewhat stressful for both the pup and his new family. Remember that you are setting the tone of night-time at your house. Unless you want to play with your pup every night at 10 p.m., midnight and 2 a.m., don't initiate the habit. Your family will thank you, and so will your pup!

PREVENTING PUPPY PROBLEMS

SOCIALISATION

Now that you have done all of the preparatory work and have helped your pup get accustomed to his new home and family, it is about time for you to have some fun! Socialising your Welsh Terrier pup gives you the opportunity to show off your new friend, and your pup gets to reap the benefits of being an adorable furry creature that people will want to pet and, in general, think is absolutely precious!

Besides getting to know his new family, your puppy should be exposed to other people, animals and situations. This will help him become well adjusted as he grows up and less prone to being timid or fearful of the new things he will encounter. Of course, he must not come into close contact with dogs you don't know well until his course of injections is fully complete.

Your pup's socialisation began with the breeder, but now it is your responsibility to continue it. The socialisation he receives until the age of 12 weeks is the most critical, as this is the time when he forms his impressions of the outside world. Special care must be taken during the eight-to-ten-

MEET THE WORLD
Thorough socialisation includes not only meeting new people but also being introduced to new experiences such as riding in the car, having his coat brushed, hearing the television, walking in a crowd—the list is endless. The more your pup experiences, and the more positive the experiences are, the less of a shock and the less frightening it will be for your pup to encounter new things.

PROPER SOCIALISATION

The socialisation period for puppies is from age 8 to 16 weeks. This is the time when puppies need to leave their birth family and take up residence with their new owners, where they will meet many new people, other pets, etc. Failure to be adequately socialised can cause the dog to grow up fearing others and being shy and unfriendly due to a lack of self-confidence.

week-old period, also known as the fear period. The interaction he receives during this time should be gentle and reassuring. Lack of socialisation, and/or negative experiences during the socialisation period, can manifest itself in fear and aggression as the dog grows up. Your puppy needs lots of positive interaction, which of course includes human contact, affection, handling and exposure to other animals.

Once your pup has received his necessary vaccinations, feel free to take him out and about (on his lead, of course). Walk him around the neighbourhood, take him on your daily errands, let people pet him, let him meet other dogs and pets, etc. Puppies do not have to try to make friends; there will be no shortage of people who will want to introduce themselves. Just make

sure that you carefully supervise each meeting. If the neighbourhood children want to say hello, for example, that is great—children and pups most often make great companions. However, sometimes an excited child can unintentionally handle a pup too roughly, or an overzealous pup can playfully nip a little too hard.

You want to make socialisation experiences positive ones. What a pup learns during this very formative stage will affect his attitude toward future encounters. You want your dog to be comfortable around everyone. A pup that

Socialisation begins at the breeder's as pups interact with their dam, their littermates and the other dogs that live there.

has a bad experience with a child may grow up to be a dog that is shy around or aggressive toward children.

CONSISTENCY IN TRAINING

Dogs, being pack animals, naturally need a leader, or else they try to establish dominance in their packs. When you welcome a dog into your family, the choice of who becomes the leader and who becomes the 'pack' is entirely up to you! Your pup's intuitive quest for dominance, coupled with the fact that it is nearly impossible to look at an adorable Welsh Terrier pup with his 'puppy-dog' eyes and not cave in, give the pup almost an unfair advantage in getting the upper hand! A pup will definitely test the waters to see what he can and cannot do.

Do not give in to those pleading eyes—stand your ground when it comes to disciplining the pup and make sure that all family members do the same. It will only confuse the pup if Mother tells him to get off the sofa when he is used to sitting up there with Father to watch the nightly news. Avoid discrepancies by having all members of the household decide on the rules before the pup even comes home…and be consistent in enforcing them! Early training shapes the dog's personality, so you cannot be unclear in what you expect.

COMMON PUPPY PROBLEMS

The best way to prevent puppy problems is to be proactive in stopping an undesirable behaviour as soon as it starts. The old saying 'You can't teach an old dog new tricks' does not necessarily hold true, but it is true that it is much easier to discourage bad behaviour in a young developing pup than to wait until the pup's bad behaviour becomes the adult dog's bad habit. There are some problems that are especially prevalent in puppies as they develop.

NIPPING

As puppies start to teethe, they feel the need to sink their teeth into anything available…unfortunately, that usually includes your fingers, arms, hair and toes. You may find this behaviour cute for the first five seconds…until you feel just how sharp those puppy teeth are. Nipping is something you want to discourage immediately and consistently with a firm 'No!' (or whatever number of firm 'Nos' it takes for him to understand that you mean business). Then, replace your finger with an appropriate chew toy. While this behaviour is merely annoying when the dog is young, it can become dangerous as your Welsh Terrier's adult teeth grow in and his jaws develop, and he continues to

PUPPY PROBLEMS
The majority of problems that are commonly seen in young pups will disappear as your dog gets older. However, how you deal with problems when he is young will determine how he reacts to discipline as an adult dog. It is important to establish who is boss (hopefully it will be you!) right away when you are first bonding with your dog. This bond will set the tone for the rest of your life together.

think it is okay to gnaw on human appendages. Your Welsh Terrier does not mean any harm with a friendly nip, but he also does not know his own strength.

CRYING/WHINING
Your pup will often cry, whine, whimper, howl or make some type of commotion when he is left alone. This is basically his way of calling out for attention to make sure that you know he is there and that you have not forgotten about him. Your puppy feels insecure when he is left alone, when you are out of the house and he is in his crate or when you are in another part of the house and he cannot see you. The noise he is making is an expression of the anxiety he feels at being alone, so he needs to be

taught that being alone is okay. You are not actually training the dog to stop making noise; rather, you are training him to feel comfortable when he is alone and thus removing the need for him to make the noise.

This is where the crate with cosy bedding and a toy comes in handy. You want to know that your pup is safe when you are not there to supervise, and you know that he will be safe in his crate rather than roaming freely about the house. In order for the pup to stay in his crate without making a fuss, he first needs to be comfortable in his crate. On that note, it is extremely important that the crate is never used as a form of punishment; this will cause the pup to view the crate as a negative place, rather than as a place of his own for safety and retreat.

Accustom the pup to the crate in short, gradually increasing time intervals in which you put him in the crate, maybe with a treat, and stay in the room with him. If he cries or makes a fuss, do not go to him, but stay in his sight. Gradually he will realise that staying in his crate is all right without your help, and it will not be so traumatic for him when you are not around. You may want to leave the radio on softly when you leave the house; the sound of human voices may be comforting to him.

Ch Vicway Modesty Blaise is a perfect example of a well-maintained Welsh Terrier in top condition. Diet, exercise and grooming are important parts of the dog's care and overall well-being.

DIETARY AND FEEDING CONSIDERATIONS

Today the choices of food for your Welsh Terrier are many and varied. There are simply dozens of brands of food in all sorts of flavours and textures, ranging from puppy diets to those for seniors. There are even hypoaller-genic and low-calorie diets available. Because your Welsh Terrier's food has a bearing on coat, health and temperament, it is essential that the most suitable diet is selected for a Welsh Terrier of his age. It is fair to say, however, that even experienced owners can be perplexed by the enormous range of foods available. Only understanding what is best for your dog will help you reach an informed decision.

Dog foods are produced in three basic types: dried, semi-moist and tinned. Dried foods are useful for the cost-conscious, for overall they tend to be less expensive than semi-moist or tinned foods. Dried foods also contain the least fat and the most preservatives. In general, tinned foods are made up of 60–70 percent water, while semi-moist ones often contain so much sugar that they are perhaps the least preferred by owners, even though their dogs seem to like them.

When selecting your dog's diet, three stages of development must be considered: the puppy stage, the adult stage and the senior or veteran stage.

PUPPY STAGE

Puppies instinctively want to suck milk from their mother's teats; a normal puppy will exhibit this behaviour just a few moments following birth. If puppies do not attempt to suckle within the first half-hour or so, they should be encouraged to do so by placing them on the nipples, having selected ones with plenty of milk. This early milk supply is

TEST FOR PROPER DIET

A good test for proper diet is the colour, odour and firmness of your dog's stool. An healthy dog usually produces three semi-hard stools per day. The stools should have no unpleasant odour. They should be the same colour from excretion to excretion.

important in providing the essential colostrum, which protects the puppies during the first eight to ten weeks of their lives. Although a mother's milk is much better than any milk formula, despite there being some excellent ones available, if the puppies do not feed, the breeder will have to feed them by hand. For those with less experience, advice from a veterinary surgeon is important so that not only the right quantity of milk is fed but also that of correct quality, fed at

DO DOGS HAVE TASTE BUDS?
Watching a dog 'wolf' or gobble his food, seemingly without chewing, leads an owner to wonder whether their dogs can taste anything. Yes, dogs have taste buds, with sensory perception of sweet, salty and sour. Puppies are born with fully mature taste buds.

suitably frequent intervals, usually every two hours during the first few days of life.

Puppies should be allowed to nurse from their mothers for about the first six weeks, although, starting around the third or fourth week, the breeder will begin to introduce small portions of suitable solid food. Most breeders like to introduce alternate milk and meat meals initially, building up to weaning time.

By the time the puppies are seven or a maximum of eight weeks old, they should be fully weaned and fed solely on a proprietary puppy food. Selection of the most suitable, good-quality diet at this time is essential, for a puppy's fastest growth rate is during the first year of life. Veterinary surgeons are usually able to offer advice in this regard and, although the frequency of meals will be reduced over time, only when a young dog has reached the age of about 12 months should an adult diet be

FEEDING TIP
You must store your dried dog food carefully. Open packages of dog food quickly lose their vitamin value, usually within 90 days of being opened. Mould spores and vermin could also contaminate the food.

fed. Puppy and junior diets should be well balanced for the needs of your dog so that, except in certain circumstances, additional vitamins, minerals and proteins will not be required.

ADULT DIETS

A dog is considered an adult when it has stopped growing, so in general the diet of a Welsh Terrier can be changed to an adult one at about 12 months of age. Again you should rely upon your veterinary surgeon or dietary specialist to recommend an acceptable maintenance diet. Major dog food manufacturers specialise in this type of food, and it is merely necessary for you to select the one best suited to your dog's needs. Active dogs may have different requirements than sedate dogs.

SENIOR DIETS

As dogs get older, their metabolism changes. The older dog usually exercises less, moves more slowly and sleeps more. This change in lifestyle and physiological performance requires a change in diet. Since these changes take place slowly, they might not be recognisable. What is easily recognisable is weight gain. By continuing to feed your dog an adult-maintenance diet when it is slowing down metabolically, your dog will gain weight. Obesity in an older dog

FOOD PREFERENCE

Selecting the best dried dog food is difficult. There is no majority consensus among veterinary scientists as to the value of nutrient analyses (protein, fat, fibre, moisture, ash, cholesterol, minerals, etc.). All agree that feeding trials are what matter, but you also have to consider the individual dog. The dog's weight, age and activity level, and what pleases his taste, all must be considered. It is probably best to take the advice of your veterinary surgeon. Every dog's dietary requirements vary, even during the lifetime of a particular dog.

If your dog is fed a good dried food, it does not require supplements of meat or vegetables. Dogs do appreciate a little variety in their diets, so you may choose to stay with the same brand but vary the flavour. Alternatively, you may wish to add a little flavoured stock to give a difference to the taste.

GRAIN-BASED DIETS

Some less expensive dog foods are based on grains and other plant proteins. While these products may appear to be attractively priced, many breeders prefer a diet based on animal proteins and believe that they are more conducive to your dog's health. Many grain-based diets rely on soy protein, which may cause flatulence (passing gas).

There are many cases, however, when your dog might require a special diet. These special requirements should only be recommended by your veterinary surgeon.

handled with a change in diet and a change in feeding schedule to give smaller portions that are more easily digested. There is no single best diet for every older dog. While many dogs do well on light or senior diets, other dogs do better on puppy diets or other special premium diets such as lamb and rice. Be sensitive to your senior Welsh Terrier's diet, as this will help control other problems that may arise with your old friend.

WATER

Just as your dog needs proper nutrition from his food, water is an essential 'nutrient' as well. Water keeps the dog's body properly hydrated and promotes normal function of the body's systems. During house-training, it is necessary to keep an eye on how much water your Welsh Terrier is drinking, but once he is reliably trained he should have access to clean fresh water at all times, especially if you feed dried food. Make certain that the dog's water bowl is clean, and change the water often.

compounds the health problems that already accompany old age.

As your dog gets older, few of his organs function up to par. The kidneys slow down and the intestines become less efficient. These age-related factors are best

EXERCISE CAUTION

Never tie a dog out to a post or tree, thinking that you are giving him exercise. This will only serve to increase aggression in the dog; with a breed that is naturally protective, tying the dog out can make the him mean.

EXERCISE

The Welsh Terrier, like all other terrier breeds, is an active dog that welcomes the chance to exercise. Two vigorous walks daily are ideal for the adult Welsh. Do not begin brisk walks with your Welsh until he is at least four months of age. As the dog reaches adulthood, the speed and distance of the walks can be increased as long as they are both kept reasonable and comfortable for both of you. A good walk will stimulate the heart rate as well as promote development of musculature.

Most importantly, your Welsh Terrier looks for structured time to spend with his owner in an active pursuit of fun. Play sessions in the garden and letting the dog run free in the garden under your supervision also are great exercise for the Welsh Terrier. Fetching games can be played indoors or out; these are excellent for giving your dog active play that he will enjoy. Chasing things that move comes naturally to dogs of all breeds, and the Welsh has strong instincts for catching things on the run. If you choose to play games outdoors, you must have a securely fenced-in garden and/or have the dog attached to at least a 8-metre (26-foot) light line for security. You want your Welsh Terrier to run, but not run away!

Bear in mind that an overweight dog should never be suddenly over-exercised; instead

DRINK, DRANK, DRUNK— MAKE IT A DOUBLE

In both humans and dogs, as well as most other living organisms, water forms the major part of nearly every body tissue. Naturally, we take water for granted, but without it, life as we know it would cease.

For dogs, water is needed to keep their bodies functioning biochemically. Additionally, water is needed to replace the water lost while panting. Unlike humans, who are able to sweat to dissipate heat, dogs must pant to cool down, thereby losing the vital water from their bodies needed to regulate their body temperatures. Humans lose electrolyte-containing products and other body-fluid components through sweating; dogs do not lose anything except water.

Water is essential always, but especially so when the weather is hot or humid or when your dog is exercising or working vigorously.

EXERCISE ALERT!
You should be careful where you exercise your dog. Many countryside areas have been sprayed with chemicals that are highly toxic to both dogs and humans. Never allow your dog to eat grass or drink from puddles on either public or private grounds, as the run-off water may contain chemicals from sprays and herbicides.

he should be encouraged to increase exercise slowly. Not only is exercise essential to keep the dog's body fit, it is essential to his mental well-being. A bored dog will find something to do, which often manifests itself in some type of destructive behaviour. In this sense, exercise is essential for the owner's mental well-being as well!

GROOMING
The Welsh Terrier has a wiry outer coat and a soft, somewhat woolly, undercoat. Neither one actually casts out or sheds; that is, the hair does not reach a certain stage of growth and fall out in profusion all over the furniture. Dead hairs are adequately removed with a good weekly brushing and combing. If the coat is not properly trimmed, the adorable puppy will become a shaggy, unattractive woolly-bully within a year, with matted lumps harbouring unwanted parasites.

Don't expect a Welsh Terrier puppy to cooperate with being groomed for more than five or ten minutes. Begin with short daily sessions and lengthen them as the puppy learns to tolerate the brushing and handling. A worthwhile investment is a small fold-up grooming table with an adjustable noose at one end to keep the dog's head up and facing the right direction. You'll get good use out of it for 12 to 14 years. It's important that the dog feel perfectly safe, so if you use something else such as an ordinary table for grooming, be sure it is steady and has a non-slip surface. Never leave any dog—puppy or adult—unsupervised on the table. A fall could cause serious injury.

The only grooming required for the first few weeks is gentle brushing and combing because the

GROOMING EQUIPMENT

How much grooming equipment you purchase will depend on how much grooming you are going to do. Here are some basics:

• Stiff bristle brush
• Slicker brush
• Palm pad
• Metal comb
• Scissors
• Stripping knife
• Electric clipper (optional)
• Rubber mat
• Dog shampoo
• Spray hose attachment
• Ear cleaner
• Cotton wipes
• Towels
• Nail clippers

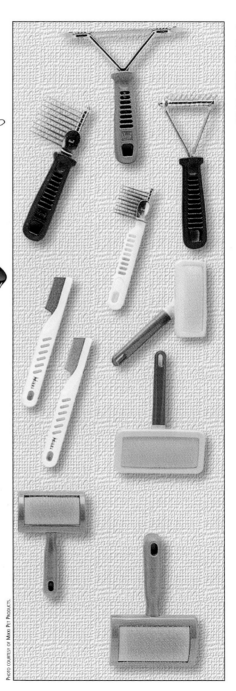

Your local pet shop will have the necessary grooming tools for you to properly care for your Welsh's coat.

primary purpose is to accustom your puppy to being handled for the real grooming to come. A thorough brushing and combing will precede every trimming session.

There are two ways to keep the Welsh looking as neat and handsome as he should. The preferred method is called plucking, or stripping, and for anyone not familiar with the process, it is best undertaken with the instruction of someone who knows exactly how to do it and can show you. It is not difficult, but it is time-consuming. Done correctly, stripping will not hurt the dog. A few hairs at a time are methodically lifted and pulled (in the direction the hair grows) using the fingers or a stripping knife.

All of the trimming is done to follow the lines of the dog. The Welsh Terrier has no frills or skirts or other enhancements to his outline. Short eyebrows are left to protect his small, deep-set eyes from nettles and twigs. All hair on the inside of the ears is removed so they fold properly for protection and are more easily kept clean. The only parts left somewhat long are the furnishings, or whiskers, on the muzzle and on the legs, and that's in part because they can take months to grow back in. The front legs are trimmed as columns, the face is styled as a rectangle and the hindquarters furnishings follow the angulation. Use photographs of show dogs for guidance.

The alternative method is to use an electric clipper, following the same pattern. A few lessons in this 'clipper control' would be a good idea since it is only easy when you've got the hang of it. Holding a noisy machine in one hand and getting the Welsh to stand still when you put this object on his head is not as easy at it looks when watching a long-time terrierman or other professional! Clipping is quicker, but it has a downside. When the hairs of both coats (wire and soft) are cut, rather than just dead hair removed, the coat often loses its

Billy poses on a grooming table. The lead is attached overhead to the table's metal arm.

deep colour. Plucking or stripping allows the strong-coloured tips of new hairs to be seen.

Of course, there is a third method—that is to pack your Welsh into the car, head to a professional groomer and pay to have someone else do it, either by stripping or clipping. No matter which method you choose, this coat work only needs to be undertaken about every three months.

For weekly grooming, you'll need two brushes. One is a terrier palm pad (also called a dolling-up pad) and the other a slicker (made with bent wires) or a stiff bristle brush. The pad is used on the furnishings, brushing against and then with the way the hair grows. The slicker or bristle brush is used on the rest of the dog. Use both gently, getting down to the skin, but not digging into it. You'll need a metal comb and a pair of scissors for trimming between the pads of the feet and around the edges of the feet, ears and so on.

All of this brushing promotes good healthy skin and removes dead hair as well as dirt and debris caught in the coat. It will also leave you with a Welsh Terrier that is handsome to look at and nice to have around the house.

Many Welsh Terriers are bathed only two or three times in their lives. Their coats shed dirt and with it any doggy odour. Most Welsh Terriers love the rain,

The palm pad is used on the furnishings, both against and with the lie of the hair.

The slicker brush is used to thoroughly brush the rest of the body.

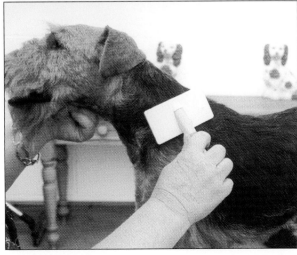

A metal comb is helpful for detangling.

The excess hair growing on the bottom of the feet, between the pads, should be carefully scissored.

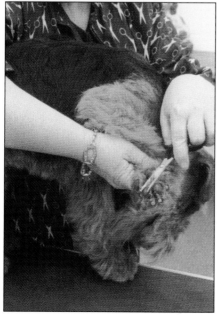

which is a good thing, considering their country of origin, but after coming in from the rain, a good towelling and a brushing are all that's needed. The wire Welsh coat is akin to a duck's back! However, if your dog rolled in muck or mud, a bath will be in order. Use a dog shampoo (people shampoos contain ingredients harmful to the dog's skin and coat) and rinse thoroughly several times. Muddy paws, and face furnishings caught up in the dinner dish, only need rinsing off as needed. Towel-dry, brush and comb all hair into place.

EAR CLEANING

The ears should be kept clean with a cotton wipe and ear powder made especially for dogs. Do not probe into the ear canal with a cotton bud, as this can cause injury. Be on the lookout for any signs of infection or ear-mite infestation. If your Welsh Terrier has been shaking his head or scratching at his ears frequently, this usually indicates a problem. If the dog's ears have an unusual odour, this is a sure sign of mite infestation or infection, and a signal to have his ears checked by the veterinary surgeon.

NAIL CLIPPING

Your Welsh Terrier should be accustomed to having his nails trimmed at an early age since nail clipping will be part of your maintenance routine throughout his life. Not only does it look nicer, but long nails can scratch someone unintentionally. Also, a long nail has a better chance of ripping and bleeding, or causing the feet to spread. A good rule of thumb is that if you can hear your dog's nails' clicking on the floor when he walks, his nails are too long.

Before you start cutting, make sure you can identify the 'quick' in each nail. The quick is a blood vessel that runs through the centre of each nail and grows rather close to the end. The quick will bleed if accidentally cut, which will be quite painful for the dog as it contains nerve endings. Keep some type of clotting agent on hand, such as a styptic pencil or styptic powder (the type used for shaving). This will stop the bleeding quickly when applied to the end of the cut nail. Do not panic if you cut the quick, just stop the bleeding and talk soothingly to your dog. Once he has calmed down, move on to the next nail. It is better to clip a little at a time, particularly with black-nailed dogs.

Hold your pup steady as you begin trimming his nails; you do not want him to make any sudden movements or run away. Talk to him soothingly and stroke him as you clip. Holding his foot in your hand, simply take off the end of each nail with one swift clip. You

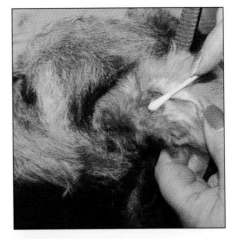

Never probe into the ear with a cotton bud; only clean that which is visible. It is safer to use a soft cotton wipe and ear cleanser for dogs.

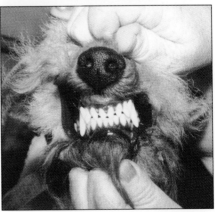

Check your dog's teeth regularly to ensure that plaque is not accumulating on the teeth and gums.

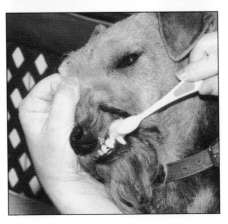

Initiate a home dental-care regimen. Use toothbrushes and toothpaste made especially for dogs.

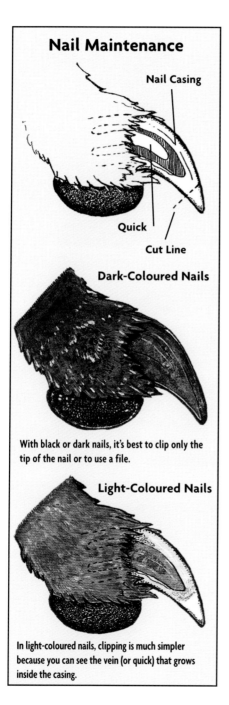

Nail Maintenance

Nail Casing

Quick

Cut Line

Dark-Coloured Nails

With black or dark nails, it's best to clip only the tip of the nail or to use a file.

Light-Coloured Nails

In light-coloured nails, clipping is much simpler because you can see the vein (or quick) that grows inside the casing.

should purchase nail clippers that are made for use on dogs; you can probably find them wherever you buy pet or grooming supplies.

TRAVELLING WITH YOUR DOG

CAR TRAVEL

You should accustom your Welsh Terrier to riding in a car at an early age. You may or may not take him in the car often, but at the very least he will need to go to

NAIL FILING

You can purchase an electric tool to grind down a dog's nails rather than cut them. Some dogs don't seem to mind the electric grinder but will object strongly to nail clippers. Talking it over with your veterinary surgeon will help you make the right choice.

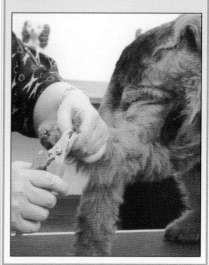

the vet and you do not want these trips to be traumatic for the dog or troublesome for you. The safest way for a dog to ride in the car is in his crate. If he uses a crate in the house, you can use the same crate for travel.

Put the pup in the crate and see how he reacts. If he seems uneasy, you can have a passenger hold him on his lap while you drive. Another option for car travel is a specially made safety harness for dogs, which straps the dog in much like a seat belt. Do not let the dog roam loose in the vehicle—this is very dangerous! If you should stop short, your dog can be thrown and injured. If the dog starts climbing on you and pestering you while you are driving, you will not be able to concentrate on the road. It is an unsafe situation for everyone— human and canine.

For long trips, be prepared to stop to let the dog relieve himself. Take with you whatever you need to clean up after him, including some paper kitchen towels and perhaps some old towelling for use should he have a toileting accident in the car or suffer from travel sickness.

AIR TRAVEL

While it is possible to take a dog on a flight within Britain, this is fairly unusual and advance permission is always required. The dog will be required to travel

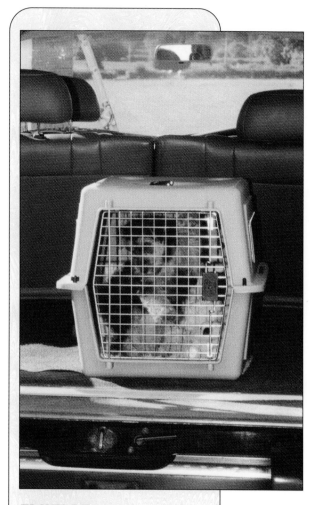

TRAVEL TIP
The most extensive travel you do with your dog may be limited to trips to the veterinary surgeon's office—or you may decide to bring him along for long distances when the family goes on holiday. Whichever the case, it is important to consider your dog's safety while travelling.

CONSIDERATIONS ABOUT BOARDING

Will your dog be exercised at least twice a day? How often during the day will the staff keep him company? Does the kennel provide a clean and secure environment? These are some of the questions you should consider when choosing a boarding kennel.

Likewise, if the staff asks you a lot of questions, this is a good sign. They need to know your dog's personality and temperament, health record, special requirements and what commands he has learned. Above all, follow your instincts. If you have a bad feeling about a kennel, even if a friend has recommended it, don't put your dog in its care.

in a fibreglass crate and you should always check in advance with the airline regarding specific requirements. To help put the dog at ease, give him one of his favourite toys in the crate. Do not feed the dog for several hours before checking in, in order to minimise his need to relieve himself. However, certain regulations specify that water must always be made available to the dog in the crate.

Make sure your dog is properly identified and that your contact information appears on his ID tags and on his crate. Animals travel in a different area of the plane than human passengers, so every rule must be strictly followed so as to prevent the risk of getting separated from your dog.

BOARDING AND HOLIDAYS

So you want to take a family holiday—and you want to include *all* members of the family. You would probably make arrangements for accommodation ahead of time anyway, but this is especially important when travelling with a dog. You do not want to make an overnight stop at the only place around for miles, only to find out that they do not allow dogs. Also, you do not want to reserve a place for your family without confirming that you are travelling with a dog, because, if it is against their policy, you may end up without a place to stay.

Alternatively, if you are travelling and choose not to bring your Welsh Terrier, you will have to make arrangements for him while you are away. Some options are to take him to a neighbour's house to stay while you are gone, to have a trusted neighbour pop in often or stay at your house or to bring your dog to a reputable boarding kennel. If you choose to board him at a kennel, you should visit in advance to see the facilities provided and where the dogs are kept. Are the dogs' areas spacious and kept clean? Talk to some of the employees and see how they treat the dogs—do they spend time with the dogs, play with

them, exercise them, etc.? Also find out the kennel's policy on vaccinations and what they require. This is for all of the dogs' safety, since there is a greater risk of diseases being passed from dog to dog when dogs are kept together.

IDENTIFICATION

Your Welsh Terrier is your valued companion and friend. That is why you always keep a close eye on him and you have made sure that he cannot escape from the garden or wriggle out of his collar and run away from you. However, accidents can happen and there may come a time when your dog unexpectedly becomes separated from you. If this unfortunate event should occur, the first thing on your mind will be finding him. Proper identification, including an ID tag, a tattoo and possibly a microchip, will increase the chances of his being returned to you safely and quickly.

Your Welsh Terrier's ID tag must be securely fastened to his everyday collar.

Training Your
WELSH TERRIER

Living with an untrained dog is a lot like owning a piano that you do not know how to play—it is a nice object to look at, but it does not do much more than that to bring you pleasure. Now try taking piano lessons, and suddenly the piano comes alive and brings forth magical sounds and rhythms that set your heart singing and your body swaying.

The same is true with your Welsh Terrier. Any dog is a big responsibility and, if not trained sensibly, may develop unacceptable behaviour that annoys you or could even cause family friction.

To train your Welsh Terrier, you may like to enrol in an obedience class. Teach your dog good manners as you learn how and why he behaves the way he does. Find out how to communicate with your dog and how to recognise and understand his communications with you. Suddenly the dog takes on a new role in your life—he is clever, interesting, well behaved and fun to be with. He demonstrates his bond of devotion to you daily. In other words, your Welsh Terrier does wonders for your ego because he constantly reminds you that you are not only his leader, you are his hero!

Those involved with teaching dog obedience and counselling owners about their dogs' behaviour have discovered some interesting facts about dog

PARENTAL GUIDANCE

Training a dog is a life experience. Many parents admit that much of what they know about raising children they learned from caring for their dogs. Dogs respond to love, fairness and guidance, just as children do. Become a good dog owner and you may become an even better parent.

ownership. For example, training dogs when they are puppies results in the highest rate of success in developing well-mannered and well-adjusted adult dogs. Training an older dog, from six months to six years of age, can produce almost equal results, providing that the owner accepts the dog's slower rate of learning capability and is willing to work patiently to help the dog succeed at developing to his fullest potential. Unfortunately, many owners of untrained adult dogs lack the patience factor, so they do not persist until their dogs are successful at learning particular behaviours.

Training a puppy aged 10 to 16 weeks (20 weeks at the most) is like working with a dry sponge in a pool of water. The pup soaks up whatever you show him and constantly looks for more things to do and learn. At this early age, his body is not yet producing

Everyone in the family should take part in the Welsh Terrier's training so that the dog will respect and obey all members of his 'pack.'

hormones, and therein lies the reason for such an high rate of success. Without hormones, he is focused on his owners and not particularly interested in investigating other places, dogs, people, etc. You are his leader: his provider of food, water, shelter and security. He latches onto you and wants to stay close. He will usually follow you from room to room, will not let you out of his sight when you are outdoors with him and will respond in like manner to the people and animals you encounter. If you greet a friend warmly, he will be happy to greet the person as well. If, however, you are hesitant or anxious about the approach of a stranger, he will respond accordingly.

THE HAND THAT FEEDS

To a dog's way of thinking, your hands are like his mouth in terms of a defence mechanism. If you squeeze him too tightly, he might just bite you because that would be his normal response. This is not aggressive biting and, although all biting should be discouraged, you need the discipline in learning how to handle your dog.

A wonderful relationship indeed...well-known Welsh Terrier breeder Judy Averis at home with one of her brood.

You usually will be able to find obedience classes within a reasonable distance from your home, but you can also do a lot to train your dog yourself. Sometimes there are classes available, but the tuition is too costly. Whatever the circumstances, the solution to training your dog without obedience classes lies within the pages of this book.

This chapter is devoted to helping you train your Welsh Terrier at home. If the recommended procedures are followed faithfully, you may expect positive results that will prove rewarding both to you and your dog.

Whether your new charge is a puppy or a mature adult, the methods of teaching and the techniques we use in training basic behaviours are the same. After all, no dog, whether puppy or adult, likes harsh or inhumane methods. All creatures, however, respond favourably to gentle motivational methods and sincere praise and encouragement. Now let us get started.

Once the puppy begins to produce hormones, his natural curiosity emerges and he begins to investigate the world around him. It is at this time when you may notice that the untrained dog begins to wander away from you and even ignore your commands to stay close. When this behaviour becomes a problem, you have two choices: get rid of the dog or train him. It is strongly urged that you choose the latter option.

REAP THE REWARDS

If you start with a normal, healthy dog and give him time, patience and some carefully executed lessons, you will reap the rewards of that training for the life of the dog. And what a life it will be! The two of you will find immeasurable pleasure in the companionship you have built together with love, respect and understanding.

TOILET TRAINING

You can train a puppy to relieve himself wherever you choose, but this must be somewhere suitable. You should bear in mind from the outset that when your puppy is old enough to go out in public places, any canine deposits must be removed at once. You will always have to carry with you a small plastic bag or 'poop-scoop.'

Outdoor training includes such surfaces as grass, soil and cement. Indoor training usually means training your dog to newspaper. When deciding on the surface and location that you will want your Welsh Terrier to use, be sure it is going to be permanent. Training your dog to grass and then changing your mind a few months later is extremely difficult for both dog and owner.

Next, choose the command you will use each and every time you want your puppy to void. 'Hurry up' and 'Toilet' are examples of commands commonly used by dog owners. Get in the habit of giving the puppy your chosen relief command before you take him out. That way, when he becomes an adult, you will be able to determine if he wants to go out when you ask him. A confirmation will be signs of interest, wagging his tail, watching you intently, going to the door, etc.

MEALTIME

Mealtime should be a peaceful time for your puppy. Do not put his food and water bowls in an high-traffic area in the house. For example, give him his own little corner where he can eat undisturbed and where he will not be underfoot. Do not allow small children or other family members to disturb the pup when he is eating.

PUPPY'S NEEDS

Puppy needs to relieve himself after play periods, after each meal, after he has been sleeping and at any time he indicates that he is looking for a place to urinate or defecate. The urinary and intestinal tract muscles of very young puppies are not fully developed. Therefore, like human babies, puppies need to relieve themselves frequently.

Take your puppy out often—

A fenced garden makes the task of house-training much easier, but only when the pup learns that it's time to 'go,' not time to explore.

both before we begin training.

Taking a new puppy home and turning him loose in your house can be compared to turning a child loose in a sports arena and telling the child that the place is all his! The sheer enormity of the place would be too much for him to handle. Instead, offer the puppy clearly defined areas where he can play, sleep, eat and live. A room of the house where the family gathers is the most obvious choice. Puppies are social animals and need to feel a part of the pack right from the start. Hearing your voice, watching you while you are doing things and smelling you nearby are all positive reinforcers that he is now a member of your pack. Usually a family room, the kitchen or a nearby adjoining breakfast area is ideal for providing safety and security for both puppy and owner.

Within the designated room, there should be a smaller area that the puppy can call his own. An

every hour for an eight-week-old, for example—and always immediately after sleeping and eating. The older the puppy, the less often he will need to relieve himself. Finally, as a mature healthy adult, he will require only three to five relief trips per day.

HOUSING

Since the types of housing and control you provide for your puppy have a direct relationship on the success of house-training, we consider the various aspects of

HONOUR AND OBEY

Dogs are the most honourable animals in existence. They consider another species (humans) as their own. They interface with you. You are their leader. Puppies perceive children to be on their level; their actions around small children are different from their behaviour around their adult masters.

CANINE DEVELOPMENT SCHEDULE

It is important to understand how and at what age a puppy develops into adulthood. If you are a puppy owner, consult the following Canine Development Schedule to determine the stage of development your puppy is currently experiencing. This knowledge will help you as you work with the puppy in the weeks and months ahead.

Period	Age	Characteristics
FIRST TO THIRD	**BIRTH TO SEVEN WEEKS**	Puppy needs food, sleep and warmth, and responds to simple and gentle touching. Needs mother for security and disciplining. Needs littermates for learning and interacting with other dogs. Pup learns to function within a pack and learns pack order of dominance. Begin socialising with adults and children for short periods. Begins to become aware of its environment.
FOURTH	**EIGHT TO TWELVE WEEKS**	Brain is fully developed. Needs socialising with outside world. Remove from mother and littermates. Needs to change from canine pack to human pack. Human dominance necessary. Fear period occurs between 8 and 12 weeks. Avoid fright and pain.
FIFTH	**THIRTEEN TO SIXTEEN WEEKS**	Training and formal obedience should begin. Less association with other dogs, more with people, places, situations. Period will pass easily if you remember this is pup's change-to-adolescence time. Be firm and fair. Flight instinct prominent. Permissiveness and over-disciplining can do permanent damage. Praise for good behaviour.
JUVENILE	**FOUR TO EIGHT MONTHS**	Another fear period sometime between 5 and 7 months of age. It passes quickly, but be cautious of fright and pain. Sexual maturity reached. Dominant traits established. Dog should understand sit, down, come and stay by now.

NOTE: THESE ARE APPROXIMATE TIME FRAMES. ALLOW FOR INDIVIDUAL DIFFERENCES IN PUPPIES.

TAKE THE LEAD
Do not carry your dog to his toilet area. Lead him there on a leash or, better yet, encourage him to follow you to the spot. If you start carrying him to his spot, you might end up doing this routine forever and your dog will have the satisfaction of having trained YOU.

alcove, a wire or fibreglass dog crate or a fenced (not boarded!) corner from which he can view the activities of his new family will be fine. The size of the area or crate is the key factor here. The area must be large enough so that the puppy can lie down and stretch out, as well as stand up, without rubbing his head on the top. At the same time, it must be small enough so that he cannot relieve himself at one end and sleep at the other without coming into contact with his droppings before he is fully trained to relieve himself outside. Dogs are, by nature, clean animals and will not remain close to their relief areas unless forced to do so. In those cases, they then become dirty dogs and usually remain that way for life.

The dog's designated area should contain clean bedding and a toy. Water must always be available, in a non-spill container, once house-training has been reliably achieved.

CONTROL
By control, we mean helping the puppy to create a lifestyle pattern that will be compatible to that of his human pack (YOU!). Just as we guide little children to learn our way of life, we must show the puppy when it is time to play, eat, sleep, exercise and even entertain himself.

Your puppy should always sleep in his crate. He should also learn that, during times of household confusion and excessive human activity, such as at breakfast when family members are preparing for the day, he can

THINK BEFORE YOU BARK

Dogs are sensitive to their masters' moods and emotions. Use your voice wisely when communicating with your dog. Never raise your voice at your dog unless you are angry and trying to correct him. 'Barking' at your dog can become as meaningless as 'dogspeak' is to you. Think before you bark!

play by himself in relative safety and comfort in his designated area. Each time you leave the puppy alone, he should understand exactly where he is to stay.

Puppies are chewers. They cannot tell the difference between lamp cords, television wires, shoes, table legs, etc. Chewing into a television wire, for example, can be fatal to the puppy, while a shorted wire can start a fire in the house. If the puppy chews on the arm of the chair when he is alone, you will probably discipline him angrily when you get home. Thus, he makes the association that your coming home means he is going to be punished. (He will not remember chewing the chair and is incapable of making the association of the discipline with his naughty deed.) Accustoming the pup to his designated area not only keeps him safe but also avoids his engaging in destructive behaviours when you are not around.

Times of excitement, such as special occasions, family parties, etc., can be fun for the puppy,

providing that he can view the activities from the security of his designated area. He is not underfoot and he is not being fed all sorts of titbits that will probably cause him stomach distress, yet he still feels a part of the fun.

SCHEDULE

A puppy should be taken to his relief area each time he is released from his designated area, after meals, after a play session and when he first awakens in the morning (at age nine weeks, this

If a fenced area is not available, you will have to be diligent in taking your dog out on his lead, at the same times each day, for him to relieve himself.

can mean 5 a.m.!). The puppy will indicate that he's ready 'to go' by circling or sniffing busily—do not misinterpret these signs. For a puppy less than ten weeks of age, a routine of taking him out every hour is necessary. As the puppy grows, he will be able to wait for longer periods of time.

Keep trips to his relief area short. Stay no more than five or

HOW MANY TIMES A DAY?	
AGE	RELIEF TRIPS
To 14 weeks	10
14–22 weeks	8
22–32 weeks	6
Adulthood	4
(dog stops growing)	

These are estimates, of course, but they are a guide to the MINIMUM opportunities a dog should have each day to relieve himself.

KEY TO SUCCESS

Success that comes by luck is usually short-lived. Success that comes by well-thought-out proven methods is often more easily achieved and permanent. This is the Success Method. It is designed to give you, the puppy owner, a simple yet proven way to help your puppy develop clean living habits and a feeling of security in his new environment.

six minutes and then return to the house. If he goes during that time, praise him lavishly and take him indoors immediately. If he does not, but he has an accident when you go back indoors, pick him up immediately, say 'No! No!' and return to his relief area. Wait a few minutes, then return to the house again. Never hit a puppy or rub his face in urine or excrement when he has had an accident!

Once indoors, put the puppy in his crate until you have had time to clean up his accident. Then, release him to the family area and watch him more closely than before. Chances are, his accident was a result of your not picking up his signal or waiting too long before offering him the opportunity to relieve himself. Never hold a grudge against the puppy for accidents.

Let the puppy learn that going

outdoors means it is time to relieve himself, not to play. Once trained, he will be able to play indoors and out and still differentiate between the times for play versus the times for relief.

Help him develop regular hours for naps, being alone, playing by himself and just resting, all in his crate. Encourage him to entertain himself while you are busy with your activities. Let him learn that having you near is comforting, but it is not your main purpose in life to provide him with undivided attention.

Each time you put your puppy in his own area, use the same command, whatever suits best. Soon he will run to his crate or special area when he hears you say those words.

Crate training provides safety for you, the puppy and the home. It also provides the puppy with a

THE SUCCESS METHOD

6 Steps to Successful Crate Training

1 Tell the puppy 'Crate time!' and place him in the crate with a small treat (a piece of cheese or half of a biscuit). Let him stay in the crate for five minutes while you are in the same room. Then release him and praise lavishly. Never release him when he is fussing. Wait until he is quiet before you let him out.

2 Repeat Step 1 several times a day.

3 The next day, place the puppy in the crate as before. Let him stay there for ten minutes. Do this several times.

4 Continue building time in five-minute increments until the puppy stays in his crate for 30 minutes with you in the room. Always take him to his relief area after prolonged periods in his crate.

5 Now go back to Step 1 and let the puppy stay in his crate for five minutes, this time while you are out of the room.

6 Once again, build crate time in five-minute increments with you out of the room. When the puppy will stay willingly in his crate (he may even fall asleep!) for 30 minutes with you out of the room, he will be ready to stay in it for several hours at a time.

TRAINING RULES

If you want to be successful in training your dog, you have four rules to obey yourself:
1. Develop an understanding of how a dog thinks.
2. Do not blame the dog for lack of communication.
3. Define your dog's personality and act accordingly.
4. Have patience and be consistent.

feeling of security, and that helps the puppy achieve self-confidence and clean habits. Remember that one of the primary ingredients in house-training your puppy is control. Regardless of your lifestyle, there will always be occasions when you will need to have a place where your dog can stay and be happy and safe. Crate training is the answer for now and in the future.

In conclusion, a few key elements are really all you need for a successful house-training method—consistency, frequency, praise, control and supervision. By following these procedures with a normal, healthy puppy, you and the puppy will soon be past the stage of 'accidents' and ready to move on to a full and rewarding life together.

ROLES OF DISCIPLINE, REWARD AND PUNISHMENT

Discipline, training one to act in accordance with rules, brings order to life. It is as simple as that. Without discipline, particularly in a group society, chaos will reign supreme and the group will eventually perish. Humans and canines are social animals and need some form of discipline in order to function effectively. They must procure food, protect their home base and their young and reproduce to keep their species going. If there were no discipline in the lives of social animals, they would eventually die from starvation and/or predation by other stronger animals.

In the case of domestic canines, discipline in their lives is needed in order for them to understand how their pack (you and other family members) functions and how they must act in order to survive.

A large humane society in an highly populated area recently surveyed dog owners regarding their satisfaction with their relationships with their dogs. People who had trained their dogs were 75% more satisfied with their pets than those who had never trained their dogs.

Dr Edward Thorndike, a psychologist, established *Thorndike's Theory of Learning*, which states that a behaviour that results in a pleasant event tends to be repeated. A behaviour that results in an unpleasant event tends not to be repeated. It is this theory upon which training methods are based today. For example, if you manipulate a dog to perform a specific behaviour and reward him for doing it, he is likely to do it again because he enjoyed the end result.

Occasionally, punishment, a penalty inflicted for an offence, is necessary. The best type of punishment often comes from an outside source. For example, a child is told not to touch the stove because he may get burned. He

TRAINING TIP

Dogs will do anything for your attention. If you reward the dog when he is calm and resting, you will develop a well-mannered dog. If, on the other hand, you greet your dog excitedly and encourage him to wrestle with you, the dog will greet you the same way and you will have an hyperactive dog on your hands.

disobeys and touches the stove. In doing so, he receives a burn. From that time on, he respects the heat of the stove and avoids contact with it. Therefore, a behaviour that results in an unpleasant event tends not to be repeated.

A good example of a dog learning the hard way is the dog who chases the house cat. He is told many times to leave the cat alone, yet he persists in teasing the cat. Then, one day, the dog begins chasing the cat but the cat turns and swipes a claw across the dog's face, leaving the dog with a painful gash on his nose. The final result is that the dog stops chasing the cat. Again, a behaviour that results in an unpleasant event tends not to be repeated.

TRAINING EQUIPMENT

COLLAR AND LEAD
For a Welsh Terrier, the collar and lead that you use for training must be one with which you are easily able to work, not too heavy for the dog and perfectly safe.

TREATS
Have a bag of treats on hand; something nutritious and easy to swallow works best. Use a soft treat, a chunk of cheese or a piece of cooked chicken rather than a dry biscuit. By the time the dog has finished chewing a dry treat, he will forget why he is being rewarded in the first place!

Using food rewards will not teach a dog to beg at the table—the only way to teach a dog to beg at the table is to give him food from the table. In training, rewarding the dog with a food treat will help him associate praise and the treats with learning new behaviours that obviously please his owner.

TRAINING BEGINS: ASK THE DOG A QUESTION
In order to teach your dog anything, you must first get his attention. After all, he cannot learn anything if he is looking away from you with his mind on something else.

To get your dog's attention, ask him 'School?' and immediately walk over to him and give him a treat as you tell him 'Good dog.' Wait a minute or two and repeat the routine, this time with a treat in your hand as you approach within a foot of the dog. Do not go directly to him, but stop about a foot short of him and hold out the treat as you ask 'School?' He will see you approaching with a treat in your hand and most likely begin walking toward you. As you meet, give him the treat and praise again.

The third time, ask the question, have a treat in your hand and walk only a short distance toward the dog so that he must walk almost all the way to

Once your pup is comfortable with his collar and lead and you're ready to start with basic commands, the sit exercise is the first you will undertake.

you. As he reaches you, give him the treat and praise again.

By this time, the dog will probably be getting the idea that if he pays attention to you, especially when you ask that question, it will pay off in treats and enjoyable activities for him. In other words, he learns that 'school' means doing great things with you that are fun and that result in positive attention for him.

Remember that the dog does not understand your verbal language; he only recognises sounds. Your question translates to a series of sounds for him, and those sounds become the signal to go to you and pay attention. The dog learns that if he does this, he will get to interact with you plus receive treats and praise.

THE BASIC COMMANDS

TEACHING SIT
Now that you have the dog's attention, attach his lead and hold it in your left hand, and hold a food treat in your right hand. Place your food hand at the dog's nose and let him lick the treat but not take it from you. Say 'Sit' and slowly raise your food hand from in front of the dog's nose up over his head so that he is looking at the ceiling. As he bends his head

DOUBLE JEOPARDY

A dog in jeopardy never lies down. He stays alert on his feet because instinct tells him that he may have to run away or fight for his survival. Therefore, if a dog feels threatened or anxious, he will not lie down. Consequently, it is important to have the dog calm and relaxed as he learns the down exercise.

upward, he will have to bend his knees to maintain his balance. As he bends his knees, he will assume a sit position. At that point, release the food treat and praise lavishly with comments such as 'Good dog! Good sit!,' etc. Remember to always praise enthusiastically, because dogs relish verbal praise from their owners and feel so proud of themselves whenever they accomplish a behaviour.

You will not use food forever in getting the dog to obey your commands. Food is only used to teach new behaviours and, once the dog knows what you want when you give a specific command, you will wean him off the food treats but still maintain the verbal praise. After all, you will always have your voice with you, and there will be many times when you have no food rewards but expect the dog to obey.

TEACHING DOWN

Teaching the down exercise is easy when you understand how the dog perceives the down position, and it is very difficult when you do not. Dogs perceive the down position as a submissive one; therefore, teaching the down exercise by using a forceful method can sometimes make the dog develop such a fear of the down that he either runs away when you say 'Down' or he attempts to snap at the person who tries to force him down.

Have the dog sit close alongside your left leg, facing in the same direction as you are. Hold the lead in your left hand and a food treat in your right. Now place your left hand lightly on the top of the dog's shoulders where they meet above the spinal cord. Do not push down on the dog's shoulders; simply rest your left hand there so you can guide the dog to lie down close to your left leg rather than to swing away from your side when he drops.

Now place the food hand at

CONSISTENCY PAYS OFF

Dogs need consistency in their feeding schedule, exercise and toilet breaks, and in the verbal commands you use. If you use 'Stay' on Monday and 'Stay here, please' on Tuesday, you will confuse your dog. Don't demand perfect behaviour during training classes and then let him have the run of the house the rest of the day. Above all, lavish praise on your pet consistently every time he does something right. The more he feels he is pleasing you, the more willing he will be to learn.

the dog's nose, say 'Down' very softly (almost a whisper), and slowly lower the food hand to the dog's front feet. When the food hand reaches the floor, begin moving it forward along the floor in front of the dog. Keep talking softly to the dog, saying things like, 'Do you want this treat? You can do this, good dog.' Your reassuring tone of voice will help calm the dog as he tries to follow the food hand in order to get the treat.

When the dog's elbows touch the floor, release the food and praise softly. Try to get the dog to maintain that down position for several seconds before you let him sit up again. The goal here is to get the dog to settle down and not feel threatened in the down position.

TEACHING STAY

It is easy to teach the dog to stay in either a sit or a down position. Again, we use food and praise during the teaching process as we help the dog to understand exactly what it is that we are expecting him to do.

To teach the sit/stay, start with the dog sitting on your left side as before and hold the lead in your left hand. Have a food treat in your right hand and place your food hand at the dog's nose. Say 'Stay' and step out on your right foot to stand directly in front of the dog, toe to toe, as he licks and nibbles the treat. Be sure to keep his head facing upward to maintain the sit position. Count to five and then swing around to stand next to the dog again with him on your left. As soon as you get back to the original position, release the food and praise lavishly.

To teach the down/stay, do the down as previously described. As

The trainer uses both verbal commands and hand signals in teaching the stay. Distance and time are increased gradually as the dog learns.

soon as the dog lies down, say 'Stay' and step out on your right foot just as you did in the sit/stay. Count to five and then return to stand beside the dog with him on your left side. Release the treat and praise as always.

Within a week to ten days, you can begin to add a bit of distance between you and your dog when you leave him. When you do, use your left hand open with the palm facing the dog as a stay signal, much the same as the hand signal a constable uses to stop traffic at a junction. Hold the food treat in your right hand as before, but this time the food will not be touching the dog's nose. He will watch the food hand and quickly learn that he is going to get that treat as soon as you return to his side.

When you can stand 1 metre away from your dog for 30 seconds, you can then begin building time and distance in both stays. Eventually, the dog can be expected to remain in the stay position for prolonged periods of time until you return to him or call him to you. Always praise lavishly when he stays.

TEACHING COME

If you make teaching 'come' an exciting experience, you should never have a 'student' that does not love the game or that fails to come when called. The secret, it seems, is never to teach the word 'come.'

At times when an owner most wants his dog to come when called, the owner is likely to be upset or anxious and he allows these feelings to come through in the tone of his voice when he calls his dog. Hearing that desperation in his owner's voice, the dog fears the results of going to him and therefore either disobeys outright or runs in the opposite direction. The secret, therefore, is to teach the dog a game and, when you want him to come to you, simply play the game. It is practically a no-fail solution!

To begin, have several members of your family take a few food treats and each go into a different room in the house. Everyone takes turns calling the dog, and each person should celebrate the dog's finding him with a treat and lots of happy praise. When a person calls the dog, he is actually inviting the dog to find him and to get a treat as a reward for 'winning.'

A few turns of the 'Where are you?' game and the dog will understand that everyone is playing the game and that each person has a big celebration awaiting the dog's success at locating him or her. Once the dog learns to love the game, simply calling out 'Where are you?' will bring him running from wherever he is when he hears that all-important question.

The come command is recognised as one of the most important things to teach a dog, but there are trainers who work with thousands of dogs and never teach the actual word 'come.' Yet these dogs will race to respond to a person who uses the dog's name followed by 'Where are you?' For example, a woman has a 12-year-old companion dog who went blind, but who never fails to locate her owner when asked, 'Where are you?'

'COME' . . . BACK

Never call your dog to come to you for a correction or scold him when he reaches you. That is the quickest way to turn a 'Come' command into 'Go away fast!' Dogs think only in the present tense, and your dog will connect the scolding with coming to you, not with the misbehaviour of a few moments earlier.

Children, in particular, love to play this game with their dogs. Children can hide in smaller places like a shower or bath, behind a bed or under a table. The dog needs to work a little bit harder to find these hiding places, but, when he does, he loves to celebrate with a treat and a tussle with a favourite youngster.

TEACHING HEEL

Heeling means that the dog walks beside the owner without pulling. It takes time and patience on the owner's part to succeed at teaching the dog that he (the owner) will not proceed unless the dog is walking calmly beside him. Neither pulling out ahead on the lead nor lagging behind is acceptable.

Begin by holding the lead in your left hand as the dog sits beside your left leg. Move the loop end of the lead to your right hand, but keep your left hand short on the lead so that it keeps the dog in close next to you.

Say 'Heel' and step forward on your left foot. Keep the dog close to you and take three steps. Stop and have the dog sit next to you in what we now call the 'heel position.' Praise verbally, but do not touch the dog. Hesitate a moment and begin again with 'Heel,' taking three steps and stopping, at which point the dog is told to sit again.

Your goal here is to have the

dog walk those three steps without pulling on the lead. Once he will walk calmly beside you for three steps without pulling, increase the number of steps you take to five. When he will walk

HEELING WELL

Teach your dog to heel in an enclosed area. Once you think the dog will obey reliably and you want to attempt advanced obedience exercises such as off-lead heeling, test him in a fenced-in area so he cannot run away.

politely beside you while you take five steps, you can increase the length of your walk to ten steps. Keep increasing the length of your stroll until the dog will walk quietly beside you without pulling as long as you want him to heel. When you stop heeling, indicate to the dog that the exercise is over by verbally praising as you pet him and say 'OK, good dog.' The 'OK' is used as a release word, meaning that the exercise is finished and the dog is free to relax.

If you are dealing with a dog who insists on pulling you around, simply 'put on your brakes' and stand your ground until the dog realises that the two of you are not going anywhere until he is beside you and moving at your pace, not his. It may take some time just standing there to convince the dog that you are the leader and that you will be the one to decide on the direction and speed of your travel.

Each time the dog looks up at you or slows down to give a slack lead between the two of you, quietly praise him and say, 'Good heel. Good dog.' Eventually, the dog will begin to respond and within a few days he will be walking politely beside you without pulling on the lead. At first, the training sessions should be kept short and very positive; soon the dog will be able to walk nicely with you for increasingly

TUG OF WALK?

If you begin teaching the heel by taking long walks and letting the dog pull you along, he misinterprets this action as an acceptable form of taking a walk. When you pull back on the lead to counteract his pulling, he reads that tug as a signal to pull even harder!

longer distances. Remember also to give the dog free time and the opportunity to run and play when you have finished heel practice.

WEANING OFF FOOD IN TRAINING

Food is used in training new behaviours. Once the dog understands what behaviour goes with a specific command, it is time to start weaning him off the food treats. At first, give a treat after each exercise. Then, start to give a treat only after every other exercise. Mix up the times when you offer a food reward and the times when you only offer praise so that the dog will never know when he is going to receive both food and praise and when he is going to receive only praise. This is called a variable ratio reward system. It proves successful because there is always the chance that the owner will produce a treat, so the dog never stops trying for that reward. No matter what, ALWAYS give verbal praise.

OBEDIENCE CLASSES

It is a good idea to enrol in an obedience class if one is available in your area. If yours is a show

A tasty titbit for a job well done! Verbal praise is even more important, so, as training progresses, you will use food rewards less frequently.

'NO' MEANS 'NO!'

Dogs do not understand our language. They can be trained to react to a certain sound, at a certain volume. If you say 'No, Oliver' in a very soft pleasant voice it will not have the same meaning as 'No, Oliver!!' when you shout it as loud as you can. You should never use the dog's name during a reprimand, just the command NO!

dog, ringcraft classes would be more appropriate. Many areas have dog clubs that offer basic obedience training as well as preparatory classes for obedience competition. There are also local dog trainers who offer similar classes.

At obedience shows, dogs can earn titles at various levels of competition. The beginning levels of obedience competition include basic behaviours such as sit, down, heel, etc. The more advanced levels of competition include jumping, retrieving, scent discrimination and signal work. The advanced levels require a dog and owner to put a lot of time and effort into their training. The titles that can be earned at these levels of competition are very prestigious.

OTHER ACTIVITIES FOR LIFE
Whether a dog is trained in the structured environment of a class or alone with his owner at home, there are many activities that can bring fun and rewards to both owner and dog once they have mastered basic control.

Teaching the dog to help out around the home, in the garden or on the farm provides great satisfaction to both dog and owner. In addition, the dog's help makes life a little easier for his owner and raises his stature as a valued companion to his family. It helps give the dog a purpose by

OBEDIENCE SCHOOL
Taking your dog to an obedience school may be the best investment in time and money you can ever make. You will enjoy the benefits for the lifetime of your dog and you will have the opportunity to meet people who have similar expectations for their companion dogs.

occupying his mind and providing an outlet for his energy.

Backpacking is an exciting and healthy activity that the dog can be taught without assistance from more than his owner. The exercise of walking and climbing is good for man and dog alike, and the bond that they develop together is

OBEDIENCE CLASS
A basic obedience beginner's class usually lasts for six to eight weeks. Dog and owner attend an hour-long lesson once a week and practise for a few minutes, several times a day, each day at home. If done properly, the whole procedure will result in a well-mannered dog and an owner who delights in living with a pet that is eager to please and enjoys doing things with his owner.

'NO' FOR A NAME

If you continually correct your dog by saying 'No,' he will soon pay no attention. There is a story that two dogs met in the park. One said to the other, 'My name is No, what is yours?'

priceless. The rule for backpacking with any dog is never to expect the dog to carry more than one-sixth of his body weight.

Be extremely careful to keep the dog on lead when hiking. Once your Welsh Terrier has put his nose down the hole of any creature that lives below ground, all his earthdog instincts will come to the fore. If hiking, not

hunting, is your aim, lead control is essential. You may note he will now be tracking and hunting in earnest on your regular walks.

If you are interested in participating in organised competition with your Welsh Terrier, there are activities other than obedience in which you and your dog can become involved. Agility is a popular sport in which dogs run through an obstacle course that includes various jumps, tunnels and other exercises to test the dog's speed and co-ordination. The owners run beside their dogs to give commands and to guide them through the course. Although competitive, the focus is on fun—it's fun to do, fun to watch and great exercise.

The Welsh Terrier is an earthdog, not a water dog! But every Welsh has individual likes and aptitudes, so find out what your dog's are and have a great time together.

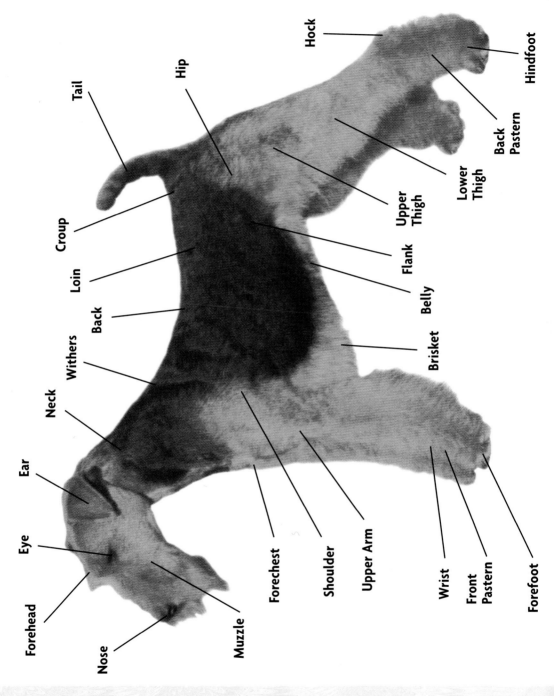

Hock

Hindfoot

Hip

Back Pastern

Tail

Lower Thigh

Upper Thigh

Croup

Flank

Loin

Belly

Back

Brisket

Withers

Neck

Ear

Eye

Forehead

Forechest

Shoulder

Upper Arm

Wrist

Front Pastern

Forefoot

Nose

Muzzle

PHYSICAL STRUCTURE OF THE WELSH TERRIER

Dogs suffer from many of the same physical illnesses as people. They might even share many of the same psychological problems. Since people usually know more about human diseases than canine maladies, many of the terms used in this chapter will be familiar but not necessarily those used by veterinary surgeons. We will use the term *x-ray*, instead of the more acceptable term *radiograph*. We will also use the familiar term *symptoms* even though dogs don't have symptoms, which are verbal descriptions of the patient's feelings; dogs have *clinical signs*. Since dogs can't speak, we have to look for clinical signs...but we still use the term *symptoms* in this book.

As a general rule, medicine is *practised*. That term is not arbitrary. Medicine is a constantly changing art as we learn more and more about genetics, electronic aids (like CAT scans) and daily laboratory advances. There are many dog maladies, like canine hip dysplasia, which are not universally treated in the same manner. Some veterinary surgeons opt for surgery more often than others do.

SELECTING A VETERINARY SURGEON

Your selection of a veterinary surgeon should not be based upon abilities and personality (as most are) but upon his convenience to your home. You want a vet who is close because you might have emergencies or need to make multiple visits for treatments. You want a vet who has services that you might require such as tattooing and grooming, as well as sophisticated pet supplies and a good reputation for ability and responsiveness. There is nothing more frustrating than having to wait a day or more to get a response from your veterinary surgeon.

All veterinary surgeons are licenced and their diplomas and/or certificates should be displayed in their waiting rooms. There are, however, many veterinary specialities that usually require further studies and internships. There are specialists in heart problems (veterinary cardiologists), skin problems (veterinary dermatologists), teeth and gum problems (veterinary dentists), eye problems (veterinary ophthalmologists) and x-rays

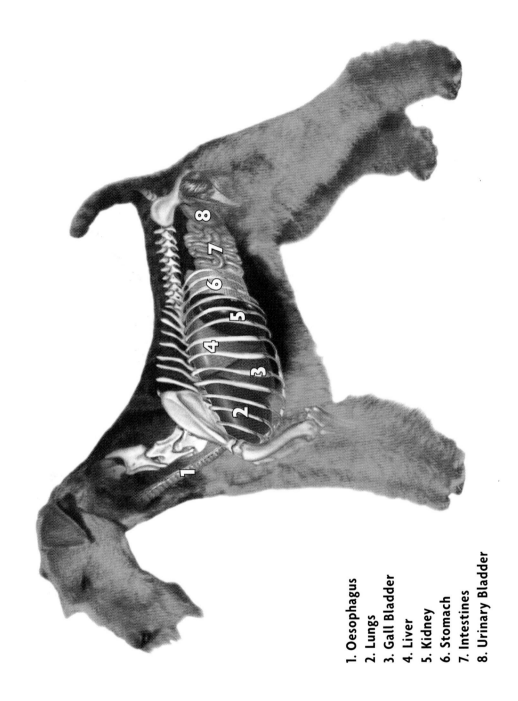

1. Oesophagus
2. Lungs
3. Gall Bladder
4. Liver
5. Kidney
6. Stomach
7. Intestines
8. Urinary Bladder

INTERNAL ORGANS OF THE WELSH TERRIER

(veterinary radiologists), as well as vets who have specialities in bones, muscles or other organs. Most veterinary surgeons do routine surgery such as neutering, stitching up wounds and docking tails for those breeds in which such is required for show purposes.

When the problem affecting your dog is serious, it is not unusual or impudent to get another medical opinion, although in Britain you are obliged to advise the vets concerned about this. You might also want to compare costs among several veterinary surgeons. Sophisticated health care and veterinary services can be very costly. It is not infrequent that important decisions are based upon financial considerations.

PREVENTATIVE MEDICINE

It is much easier, less costly and more effective to practise preventative medicine than to fight bouts of illness and disease. Properly bred puppies come from parents who were selected based upon their genetic disease profiles. Their mothers should have been vaccinated, free of all internal and external parasites and properly nourished. The dam can pass on disease resistance to her puppies, which can last for eight to ten weeks, but she can also pass on parasites and many infections. For these reasons, a visit to the veterinary surgeon who cared for the dam is recommended.

Breakdown of Veterinary Income by Category

2%	Dentistry
4%	Radiology
12%	Surgery
15%	Vaccinations
19%	Laboratory
23%	Examinations
25%	Medicines

A typical American vet's income, categorised according to services performed. This survey dealt with small-animal (pets) practices.

VACCINATION SCHEDULING
Most vaccinations are given by injection and should only be done by a veterinary surgeon. Both he and you should keep records of the date of the injection, the identification of the vaccine and the amount given. Some vets give a first vaccination at eight weeks, but most dog breeders prefer the course not to commence until about ten weeks to avoid negating any antibodies passed on by the dam. The vaccination scheduling is usually based on a 15-day cycle. You must take your vet's advice regarding when to vaccinate, as this may differ according to the vaccine used. Most vaccinations immunize your puppy against viruses.

The usual vaccines contain immunizing doses of several different viruses such as distemper, parvovirus, parain-

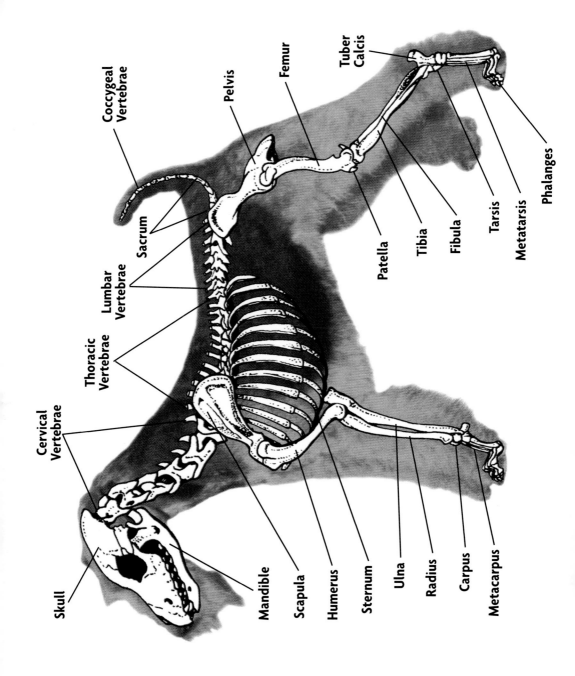

Coccygeal Vertebrae

Pelvis

Femur

Tuber Calcis

Phalanges

Sacrum

Tibia

Fibula

Tarsis

Metatarsis

Lumbar Vertebrae

Patella

Thoracic Vertebrae

Cervical Vertebrae

Skull

Mandible

Scapula

Humerus

Sternum

Ulna

Radius

Carpus

Metacarpus

SKELETAL STRUCTURE OF THE WELSH TERRIER

fluenza and hepatitis, although some veterinary surgeons recommend separate vaccines for each disease. There are other vaccines available when the puppy is at risk. You should rely upon professional advice. This is especially true for the booster-shot programme. Most vaccination programmes require a booster when the puppy is a year old and once a year thereafter. In some cases, circumstances may require more or less frequent immunizations. Kennel cough, more formally known as tracheobronchitis, is treated with a vaccine that is sprayed into the dog's nostrils. Kennel cough is usually included in routine vaccination, but this is often not so effective as for other major diseases.

WEANING TO FIVE MONTHS OLD

Puppies should be weaned by the time they are about two months old. A Welsh puppy that remains for at least nine weeks with its mother and littermates usually adapts better to other dogs and people later in life. Some new owners have their puppies examined by veterinary surgeons immediately, which is a good idea. Vaccination programmes usually begin when the puppy is very young.

The puppy will have its teeth examined, and have its skeletal

HEALTH AND VACCINATION SCHEDULE

AGE IN WEEKS:	6TH	8TH	10TH	12TH	14TH	16TH	20-24TH	52ND
Worm Control	✔	✔	✔	✔	✔	✔	✔	
Neutering								✔
Heartworm		✔		✔		✔	✔	
Parvovirus	✔		✔		✔		✔	✔
Distemper		✔		✔		✔		✔
Hepatitis		✔		✔		✔		✔
Leptospirosis								✔
Parainfluenza	✔		✔		✔			✔
Dental Examination		✔					✔	✔
Complete Physical		✔					✔	✔
Coronavirus				✔			✔	✔
Kennel Cough	✔							
Hip Dysplasia								✔
Rabies							✔	

Vaccinations are not instantly effective. It takes about two weeks for the dog's immune system to develop antibodies. Most vaccinations require annual booster shots. Your veterinary surgeon should guide you in this regard.

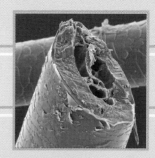

Normal hairs of a dog enlarged 200 times original size. The cuticle (outer covering) is clean and healthy. Unlike human hair that grows from the base, a dog's hair also grows from the end. Damaged hairs and split ends, illustrated above.

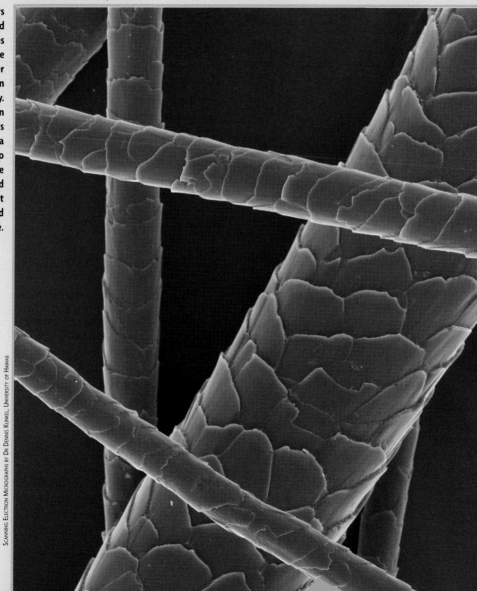

SCANNING ELECTRON MICROGRAPHS BY DR DENNIS KUNKEL, UNIVERSITY OF HAWAII

DISEASE REFERENCE CHART

	What is it?	What causes it?	Symptoms
Leptospirosis	Severe disease that affects the internal organs; can be spread to people.	A bacterium, which is often carried by rodents, that enters through mucous membranes and spreads quickly throughout the body.	Range from fever, vomiting and loss of appetite in less severe cases to shock, irreversible kidney damage and possibly death in most severe cases.
Rabies	Potentially deadly virus that infects warm-blooded mammals. Not seen in United Kingdom.	Bite from a carrier of the virus, mainly wild animals.	1st stage: dog exhibits change in behaviour, fear. 2nd stage: dog's behaviour becomes more aggressive. 3rd stage: loss of coordination, trouble with bodily functions.
Parvovirus	Highly contagious virus, potentially deadly.	Ingestion of the virus, which is usually spread through the faeces of infected dogs.	Most common: severe diarrhoea. Also vomiting, fatigue, lack of appetite.
Kennel cough	Contagious respiratory infection.	Combination of types of bacteria and virus. Most common: *Bordetella bronchiseptica* bacteria and parainfluenza virus.	Chronic cough.
Distemper	Disease primarily affecting respiratory and nervous system.	Virus that is related to the human measles virus.	Mild symptoms such as fever, lack of appetite and mucous secretion progress to evidence of brain damage, 'hard pad.'
Hepatitis	Virus primarily affecting the liver.	Canine adenovirus type I (CAV-1). Enters system when dog breathes in particles.	Lesser symptoms include listlessness, diarrhoea, vomiting. More severe symptoms include 'blue-eye' (clumps of virus in eye).
Coronavirus	Virus resulting in digestive problems.	Virus is spread through infected dog's faeces.	Stomach upset evidenced by lack of appetite, vomiting, diarrhoea.

conformation and general health checked prior to certification by the veterinary surgeon. Puppies in certain breeds may have problems with their kneecaps, cataracts and

VACCINE ALLERGIES

Vaccines do not work all the time. Sometimes dogs are allergic to them and many times the antibodies, which are supposed to be stimulated by the vaccine, just are not produced. You should keep your dog in the veterinary clinic for an hour after it is vaccinated to be sure there are no allergic reactions.

The grass can harbour insects, parasites, pollen and other irritants that can affect your Welsh Terrier. Check his skin and coat often for any signs of abnormality.

other eye problems, heart murmurs or undescended testicles. They may also have personality problems, and your veterinary surgeon might have training in temperament evaluation.

FIVE TO TWELVE MONTHS OF AGE
Unless you intend to breed or show your dog, neutering the puppy at six months of age is recommended. Discuss this with your veterinary surgeon. Neutering/spaying has proven to be extremely beneficial to male and female puppies, respectively. Besides eliminating the possibility of pregnancy, it inhibits (but does not prevent) breast cancer in bitches and prostate cancer in male dogs. Under no circumstances should a bitch be spayed prior to her first season.

Your veterinary surgeon should provide your puppy with a thorough dental evaluation at six months of age, ascertaining whether all the permanent teeth have erupted properly. An home dental care regimen should be initiated at six months, including brushing weekly and providing good dental devices (such as nylon bones). Regular dental care promotes healthy teeth, fresh breath and a longer life.

ONE TO SEVEN YEARS
Once a year, your fully-grown dog should visit the vet for an

PUPPY VACCINATIONS
Your veterinary surgeon will probably recommend that your puppy be vaccinated before you take him outside. There are airborne diseases, parasite eggs in the grass and unexpected visits from other dogs that might be dangerous to your puppy's health.

examination and vaccination boosters, if needed. Some vets recommend blood tests, a thyroid level check and a dental evaluation to accompany these annual visits. A thorough clinical evaluation by the vet can provide critical background information for your dog. Blood tests are often performed at one year of age, and dental examinations around the third or fourth birthday. In the long run, quality preventative care for your pet can save money, teeth and lives.

MORE THAN VACCINES
Vaccinations help prevent your new puppy from contracting diseases, but they do not cure diseases. Proper nutrition as well as parasite control keep your dog healthy and less susceptible to many dangerous diseases. Remember that your dog depends on you to ensure his well-being.

DO YOU KNOW ABOUT HIP DYSPLASIA?

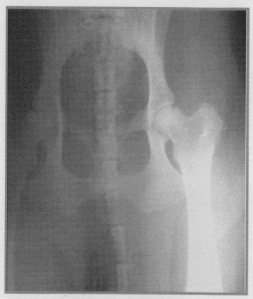

X-ray of a dog with 'Good' hips.

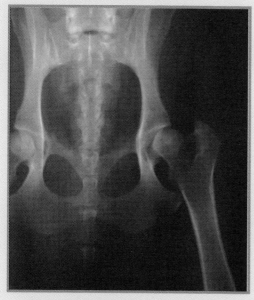

X-ray of a dog with 'Moderate' dysplastic hips.

Hip dysplasia is a fairly common condition found in pure-bred dogs. When a dog has hip dysplasia, its hind leg has an incorrectly formed hip joint. By constant use of the hip joint, it becomes more and more loose, wears abnormally and may become arthritic.

Hip dysplasia can only be confirmed with an x-ray, but certain symptoms may indicate a problem. Your dog may have a hip dysplasia problem if it walks in a peculiar manner, hops instead of smoothly runs, uses its hind legs in unison (to keep the pressure off the weak joint), has trouble getting up from a prone position or always sits with both legs together on one side of its body.

As the dog matures, it may adapt well to life with a bad hip, but in a few years the arthritis develops and many dogs with hip dysplasia become cripples.

Hip dysplasia is considered an inherited disease and only can be diagnosed definitively when the dog is two years old. Some experts claim that a special diet might help your puppy outgrow the bad hip, but the usual treatments are surgical. The removal of the pectineus muscle, the removal of the round part of the femur, reconstructing the pelvis and replacing the hip with an artificial one are all surgical interventions that are expensive, but they are usually very successful. Follow the advice of your veterinary surgeon.

SKIN PROBLEMS

Veterinary surgeons are consulted by dog owners for skin problems more than for any other group of diseases or maladies. Dogs' skin is almost as sensitive as human skin, and both suffer from almost the same ailments (though the occurrence of acne in dogs is rare!). For this reason, veterinary dermatology has developed into a speciality practised by many veterinary surgeons.

Since many skin problems have visual symptoms that are almost identical, it requires the skill of an experienced veterinary dermatologist to identify and cure many of the more severe skin disorders. Pet shops sell many treatments for skin problems, but most of the treatments are directed at the symptoms and not the underlying problem(s). If your dog is suffering from a skin disorder, you should seek professional assistance as quickly as possible. As with all diseases, the earlier a problem is identified and treated, the more successful is the cure.

AUTO-IMMUNE SKIN CONDITIONS

An auto-immune skin condition is commonly referred to as a condition in which a person (or dog) is 'allergic' to him- or herself, while an allergy is usually an inflammatory reaction to an outside stimulus. Auto-immune diseases cause serious damage to the tissues that are involved.

The best known auto-immune disease is lupus, which affects people as well as dogs. The symptoms are variable and may affect the kidneys, bones, blood chemistry and skin. It can be fatal to both dogs and humans, though it is not thought to be transmissible. It is usually successfully treated with cortisone, prednisone or a similar corticosteroid, but extensive use of these drugs can have harmful side effects.

AIRBORNE ALLERGIES

Just as humans have hay fever, rose fever and other fevers from which they suffer during the pollinating season, many dogs suffer from the same allergies, and these commonly plague some Welsh Terriers. When the pollen count is high, your dog might suffer, but don't expect him to sneeze and have a runny nose like a human would. Dogs react to pollen allergies the same way they react to fleas—they scratch and bite themselves.

Dogs, like humans, can be tested for allergens. Discuss the testing with your veterinary dermatologist.

FOOD PROBLEMS

FOOD ALLERGIES

Dogs are allergic to many foods that are best-sellers and highly recommended by breeders and veterinary surgeons. Changing the brand of food that you buy may not eliminate the problem if the element to which the dog is allergic is contained in the new brand.

Recognising a food allergy is difficult. Humans vomit or have rashes when they eat a food to which they are allergic. Dogs neither vomit nor (usually) develop rashes. They react in the same manner as they would to an airborne or flea allergy; they itch, scratch and bite, thus making the diagnosis extremely difficult. While pollen allergies and parasite bites are usually seasonal, food allergies are year-round problems.

FOOD INTOLERANCE
Food intolerance is the inability of the dog to completely digest certain foods. For example, puppies that may have done very well on their mother's milk may not do well on cow's milk. The results of food intolerance may be evident in loose bowels, passing gas and stomach pains. These are the only obvious symptoms of food intolerance, which makes diagnosis difficult.

TREATING FOOD PROBLEMS
It is possible to handle food allergies and food intolerance yourself. Start by putting your dog on a diet that he has never had. Obviously, if the dog has

never eaten this new food, he can't have been allergic or intolerant of it. Start with a single ingredient that is not in the dog's diet at the present time. Ingredients like chopped beef or fish are common in dogs' diets, so try something more exotic like rabbit, pheasant or even just vegetables. Keep the dog on this diet (with no additives) for a month. If the symptoms of food allergy or intolerance disappear, it is quite likely that your dog has a food allergy.

Don't think that the single ingredient cured the problem. You still must find a suitable diet and ascertain which ingredient in the old diet was objectionable. This is most easily done by adding ingredients to the new diet one at a time. Let the dog stay on the modified diet for a month before you add another ingredient. Eventually, you will determine the ingredient that caused the adverse reaction.

An alternative method is to carefully study the ingredients in the diet to which your dog is allergic or intolerant. Identify the main ingredient in this diet and eliminate the main ingredient by buying a different food that does not have that ingredient. Keep experimenting until the symptoms disappear after one month on the new diet.

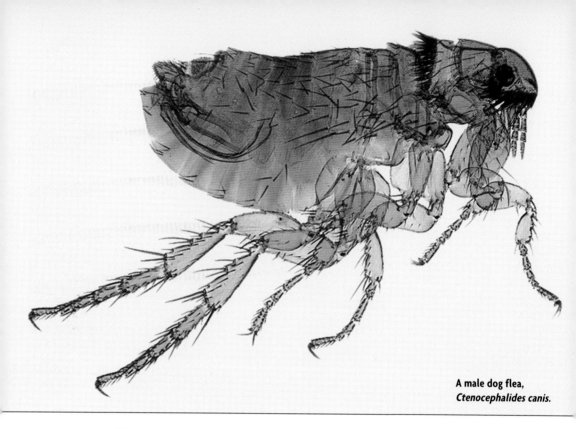

A male dog flea,
Ctenocephalides canis.

EXTERNAL PARASITES

FLEAS

Of all the problems to which dogs are prone, none is more well known and frustrating than fleas. Flea infestation is relatively simple to cure but difficult to prevent. Parasites that are harboured inside the body are a bit more difficult to eradicate but they are easier to control.

To control flea infestation, you have to understand the flea's life cycle. Fleas are often thought of as a summertime problem, but centrally heated homes have changed the patterns and fleas can be found at any time of the year.

The most effective method of flea control is a two-stage approach: one stage to kill the adult fleas, and the other to control the development of pre-adult fleas. Unfortunately, no single active ingredient is effective against all stages of the life cycle.

LIFE CYCLE STAGES

During its life, a flea will pass through four life stages: egg, larva, pupa and adult. The adult stage is the most visible and irritating stage of the flea life cycle, and this is why the majority of flea-control products concentrate on this stage. The fact is that adult fleas account for only 1% of the total flea population, and the other 99% exist in pre-adult stages, i.e. eggs, larvae and pupae. The pre-adult stages are barely visible to the naked eye.

THE LIFE CYCLE OF THE FLEA

Eggs are laid on the dog, usually in quantities of about 20 or 30, several times a day. The adult female flea must have a blood meal before each egg-laying session. When first laid, the eggs will cling to the dog's hair, as the eggs are still moist. However, they will quickly dry out and fall from the dog, especially if the dog moves around or scratches. Many eggs will fall off in the dog's favourite area or an area in which he spends a lot of time, such as his bed.

Once the eggs fall from the dog onto the carpet or furniture, they will hatch into larvae. This takes from one to ten days. Larvae are not particularly mobile and will usually travel only a few

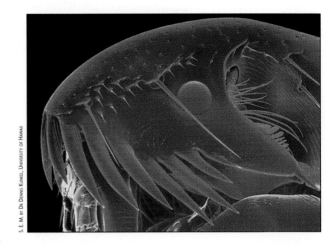

S. E. M. BY DR DENNIS KUNKEL, UNIVERSITY OF HAWAII

Magnified head of a dog flea, *Ctenocephalides canis*, colorized for effect.

inches from where they hatch. However, they do have a tendency to move away from light and heavy traffic—under furniture and behind doors are common places to find high quantities of flea larvae.

The flea larvae feed on dead organic matter, including adult flea faeces, until they are ready to change into adult fleas. Fleas will usually remain as larvae for around seven days. After this period, the larvae will pupate into protective pupae. While inside the pupae, the larvae will undergo metamorphosis and change into adult fleas. This can take as little time as a few days, but the adult fleas can remain inside the pupae waiting to hatch for up to two years. The pupae are signalled to hatch by certain stimuli, such as physical pressure—the pupae's being stepped on, heat from an animal's lying on the pupae or

FLEA KILLERS

Flea-killers are poisonous. You should not spray these toxic chemicals on areas of a dog's body that he licks, on his genitals or on his face. Flea killers taken internally are a better answer, but check with your vet in case internal therapy is not advised for your dog.

The dog flea is the most common parasite found on pet dogs.

S. E. M. BY DR DENNIS KUNKEL, UNIVERSITY OF HAWAII

increased carbon-dioxide levels and vibrations—indicating that a suitable host is available.

Once hatched, the adult flea must feed within a few days. Once the adult flea finds an host, it will not leave voluntarily. It only becomes dislodged by grooming or the host animal's scratching. The adult flea will remain on the host for the duration of its life unless forcibly removed.

Dwight R Kuhn's magnificent action photo, showing a flea jumping from a dog's back.

PHOTO BY DWIGHT R KUHN

TREATING THE ENVIRONMENT AND THE DOG

Treating fleas should be a two-pronged attack. First, the environment needs to be treated; this includes carpets and furniture, especially the dog's bedding and areas underneath furniture. The environment should be treated with an household spray containing an Insect Growth Regulator (IGR) and an insecticide to kill the adult fleas. Most IGRs are effective against eggs and larvae; they actually mimic the fleas' own hormones and stop the eggs and larvae from developing into adult fleas. There are currently no treatments available to attack the pupa stage of the life cycle, so the adult insecticide is used to kill the newly hatched adult fleas before they find an host. Most IGRs are active for many months, while adult insecticides are only active for a few days.

When treating with an household spray, it is a good idea to vacuum before applying the product. This stimulates as many pupae as possible to hatch into adult fleas. The vacuum cleaner should also be treated with an insecticide to prevent the eggs and larvae that have been hoovered into the vacuum bag from hatching.

The second stage of treatment is to apply an adult insecticide to

EN GARDE: CATCHING FLEAS OFF GUARD!

Consider the following ways to arm yourself against fleas:

- Add a small amount of pennyroyal or eucalyptus oil to your dog's bath. These natural remedies repel fleas.
- Supplement your dog's food with fresh garlic (minced or grated) and a hearty amount of brewer's yeast, both of which ward off fleas.
- Use a flea comb on your dog daily. Submerge fleas in a cup of bleach to kill them quickly.
- Confine the dog to only a few rooms to limit the spread of fleas in the home.
- Vacuum daily...and get all of the crevices! Dispose of the bag every few days until the problem is under control.
- Wash your dog's bedding daily. Cover cushions where your dog sleeps with towels, and wash the towels often.

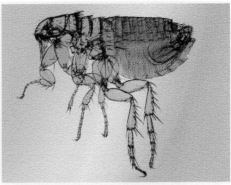

PHOTO BY JEAN CLAUDE REVY/PHOTOTAKE

A LOOK AT FLEAS

Fleas have been around for millions of years and have adapted to changing host animals. They are able to go through a complete life cycle in less than one month or they can extend their lives to almost two years by remaining as pupae or cocoons. They do not need blood or any other food for up to 20 months.

They have been measured as being able to jump 300,000 times and can jump 150 times their length in any direction, including straight up. Those are just a few of the reasons why they are so successful in infesting a dog!

THE LIFE CYCLE OF THE FLEA

Eggs

Larvae

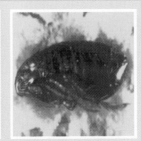

Pupa

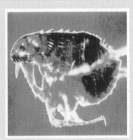

Adult

Photos courtesy of Fleabusters® Rx for fleas.

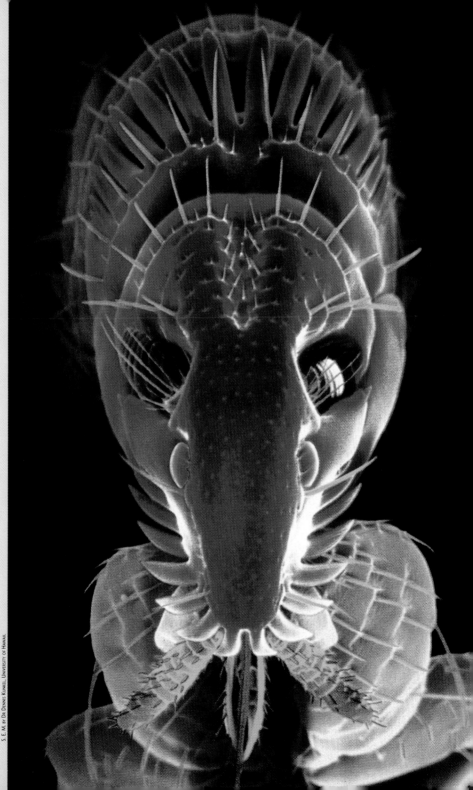

A scanning electron micrograph of a dog or cat flea, *Ctenocephalides,* magnified more than 100x. This image has been colorized for effect.

S. E. M. BY DR. DENNIS KUNKEL, UNIVERSITY OF HAWAII.

the dog. Traditionally, this would be in the form of a collar or a spray, but more recent innovations include digestible insecticides that poison the fleas when they ingest the dog's blood. Alternatively, there are drops that, when placed on the back of the animal's neck, spread throughout the fur and skin to kill adult fleas.

INSECT GROWTH REGULATOR (IGR)

Two types of products should be used when treating fleas—a product to treat the pet and a product to treat the home. Adult fleas represent less than 1% of the flea population. The pre-adult fleas (eggs, larvae and pupae) represent more than 99% of the flea population and are found in the environment; it is in the case of pre-adult fleas that products containing an Insect Growth Regulator (IGR) should be used in the home.

IGRs are a new class of compounds used to prevent the development of insects. They do not kill the insect outright, but instead use the insect's biology against it to stop it from completing its growth. Products that contain methoprene are the world's first and leading IGRs. Used to control fleas and other insects, this type of IGR will stop flea larvae from developing and protect the house for up to seven months.

TICKS AND MITES

Though not as common as fleas, ticks and mites are found all over the tropical and temperate world. They don't bite, like fleas; they harpoon. They dig their sharp proboscis (nose) into the dog's skin and drink the blood. Their only food and drink is dog's blood. Dogs can get Lyme disease, Rocky Mountain spotted fever (normally found in the US only), paralysis and many other diseases from ticks and mites. They may live where fleas are found and they like to hide in cracks or seams in walls wherever dogs live. They are controlled the same way fleas are controlled.

The dog tick, *Dermacentor variabilis*, may well be the most common dog tick in many geographical areas, especially those areas where the climate is hot and humid. Most dog ticks

A brown dog tick, *Rhipicephalus sanguineus*, is an uncommon but annoying tick found on dogs.

The head of a dog tick, *Dermacentor variabilis*, enlarged and colorized for effect.

PHOTO BY DR. DENNIS KUNKEL, UNIVERSITY OF HAWAII

DEER TICK CROSSING

The great outdoors may be fun for your dog, but it also is an home to dangerous ticks. Deer ticks carry a bacterium known as *Borrelia burgdorferi* and are most active in the autumn and spring. When infections are caught early, penicillin and tetracycline are effective antibiotics, but, if left untreated, the bacteria may cause neurological, kidney and cardiac problems as well as long-term trouble with walking and painful joints.

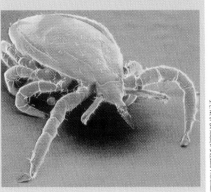

S. E. M. BY DR. ANDREW SPIELMAN/PHOTOTAKE

have life expectancies of a week to six months, depending upon climatic conditions. They can neither jump nor fly, but they can crawl slowly and can range up to 5 metres (16 feet) to reach a sleeping or unsuspecting dog.

Human lice look like dog lice; the two are closely related.

PHOTO BY DWIGHT R KUHN

MANGE

Mites cause a skin irritation called mange. Some mites are contagious, like *Cheyletiella*, ear mites, scabies and chiggers. Mites that cause ear-mite infestations are usually controlled with

Lindane, which can only be administered by a vet, followed by Tresaderm at home. It is essential that your dog be treated for mange as quickly as possible because some forms of mange are transmissible to people.

Opposite page:
The dog tick, *Dermacentor variabilis*, is probably the most common tick found on dogs. Look at the strength in its eight legs! No wonder it's hard to detach them.

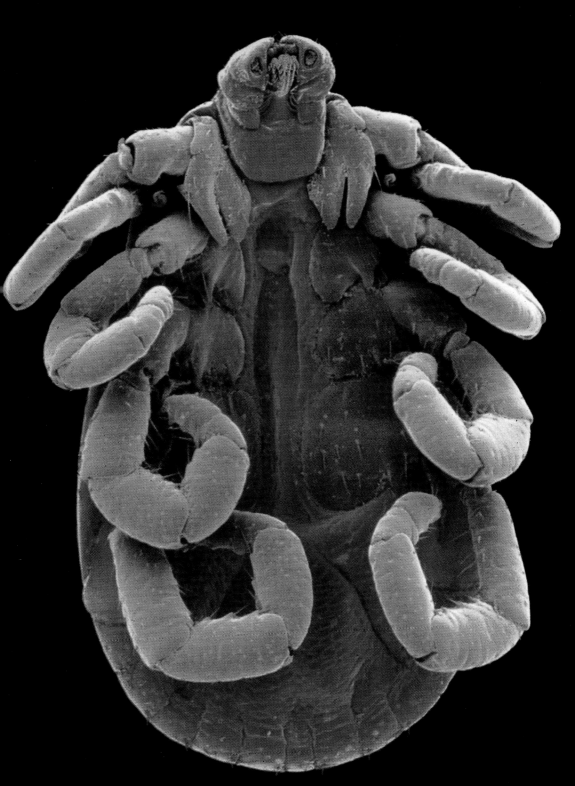

The mange mite, *Psoroptes bovis*.

INTERNAL PARASITES

Most animals—fishes, birds and mammals, including dogs and humans—have worms and other parasites that live inside their bodies. According to Dr Herbert R Axelrod, the fish pathologist, there are two kinds of parasites: dumb and smart. The smart parasites live in peaceful cooperation with their hosts (symbiosis), while the dumb parasites kill their hosts. Most of the worm infections are relatively easy to control. If they are not controlled, they weaken the host dog to the point that other medical problems occur, but they do not kill the host as dumb parasites would.

ROUNDWORMS

The roundworms that infect dogs are known scientifically as *Toxocara canis*. They live in the dog's intestines. The worms shed eggs continually. It has been estimated that a dog produces about 150 grammes of faeces every day. Each gramme of faeces averages 10,000–12,000 eggs of roundworms. There are no known areas in which dogs roam that do not contain roundworm eggs. The greatest danger of roundworms is

ROUNDWORMS

Average-size dogs can pass 1,360,000 roundworm eggs every day. For example, if there were only 1 million dogs in the world, the world would be saturated with 1,300 metric tonnes of dog faeces. These faeces would contain 15,000,000,000 roundworm eggs.

Up to 31% of home gardens and children's play boxes in the US contain roundworm eggs.

Flushing dog's faeces down the toilet is not a safe practice because the usual sewage treatments do not destroy roundworm eggs.

Infected puppies start shedding roundworm eggs at 3 weeks of age. They can be infected by their mother's milk.

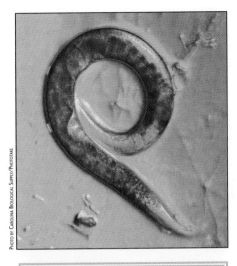

PHOTO BY CAROLINA BIOLOGICAL SUPPLY/PHOTOTAKE

The roundworm *Rhabditis* can infect both dogs and humans.

that they infect people too! It is wise to have your dog tested regularly for roundworms.

Pigs also have roundworm infections that can be passed to humans and dogs. The typical roundworm parasite is called *Ascaris lumbricoides.*

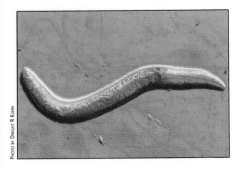

PHOTO BY DWIGHT R KUHN

DEWORMING

Ridding your puppy of worms is *very important* because certain worms that puppies carry, such as tapeworms and roundworms, can infect humans.

Breeders initiate deworming programmes at or about four weeks of age. The routine is repeated every two or three weeks until the puppy is three months old. The breeder from whom you obtained your puppy should provide you with the complete details of the deworming programme.

Your veterinary surgeon can prescribe and monitor the programme of deworming for you. The usual programme is treating the puppy every 15–20 days until the puppy is positively worm-free. It is advised that you only treat your puppy with drugs that are recommended professionally.

The common roundworm, *Ascaris lumbricoides.*

Left: *Ancylostoma caninum* are uncommonly found in pet or show dogs in Britain.

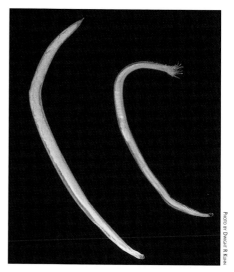

Right: Male and female hookworms.

HOOKWORMS

The worm *Ancylostoma caninum* is commonly called the dog hookworm. It is also dangerous to humans and cats. It has teeth by which it attaches itself to the intestines of the dog. It changes the site of its attachment about six times a day and the dog loses blood from each detachment, possibly causing iron-deficiency anaemia. Hookworms are easily purged from the dog with many medications. Milbemycin oxime, which also serves as an heartworm preventative in

Collies, can be used for this purpose.

In Britain the 'temperate climate' hookworm (*Uncinaria stenocephala*) is rarely found in pet or show dogs, but can occur in hunting packs, racing Greyhounds and sheepdogs because the worms can be prevalent wherever dogs are exercised regularly on grassland.

TAPEWORMS

There are many species of tapeworm, all of which are carried by fleas! The dog eats the flea and starts the tapeworm cycle. Humans can also be infected with tapeworms—so don't eat fleas! Fleas are so small that your dog could pass them onto your hands, your plate or your food and thus make it possible for you to ingest a flea that is carrying tapeworm eggs.

The infective stage of the hookworm larva.

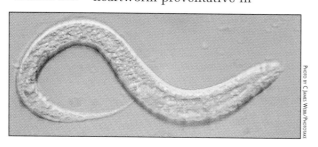

TAPEWORMS

Humans, rats, squirrels, foxes, coyotes, wolves and domestic dogs are all susceptible to tapeworm infection. Except in humans, tapeworms are usually not a fatal infection. Infected individuals can harbour 1000 parasitic worms.

Tapeworms have two sexes—male and female (many other worms have only one sex—male and female in the same worm).

If dogs eat infected rats or mice, they get the tapeworm disease. One month after attaching to a dog's intestine, the worm starts shedding eggs. These eggs are infective immediately. Infective eggs can live for a few months without an host animal.

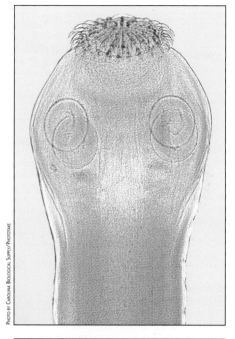

PHOTO BY CAROLINA BIOLOGICAL SUPPLY/PHOTOTAKE

The head and rostellum (the round prominence on the scolex) of a tapeworm, which infects dogs and humans.

While tapeworm infection is not life-threatening in dogs (smart parasite!), it can be the cause of a very serious liver disease for humans. About 50 percent of the humans infected with *Echinococcus multilocularis*, a type of tapeworm that causes alveolar hydatis, perish.

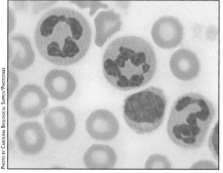

PHOTO BY CAROLINA BIOLOGICAL SUPPLY/PHOTOTAKE

Magnified heartworm larvae, *Dirofilaria immitis.*

PHOTO BY J E HAYDEN, RBP/PHOTOTAKE

Heartworm, *Dirofilaria immitis.*

First Aid at a Glance

Burns
Place the affected area under cool water; use ice if only a small area is burnt.

Insect bites
Apply ice to relieve swelling; antihistamine dosed properly.

Animal bites
Clean any bleeding area; apply pressure until bleeding subsides; go to the vet.

Spider bites
Use cold compress and a pressurised pack to inhibit venom's spreading.

Antifreeze poisoning
Induce vomiting with hydrogen peroxide. Seek *immediate* veterinary help!

Fish hooks
Removal best handled by vet; hook must be cut in order to remove.

Snake bites
Pack ice around bite; contact vet quickly; identify snake for proper antivenin.

Car accident
Move dog from roadway with blanket; seek veterinary aid.

Shock
Calm the dog, keep him warm; seek immediate veterinary help.

Nosebleed
Apply cold compress to the nose; apply pressure to any visible abrasion.

Bleeding
Apply pressure above the area; treat wound by applying a cotton pack.

Heat stroke
Submerge dog in cold bath; cool down with fresh air and water; go to the vet.

Frostbite/Hypothermia
Warm the dog with a warm bath, electric blankets or hot water bottles.

Abrasions
Clean the wound and wash out thoroughly with fresh water; apply antiseptic.

 Remember: an injured dog may attempt to bite an helping hand from fear and confusion. Always muzzle the dog before trying to offer assistance.

HEARTWORMS

Heartworms are thin, extended worms up to 30 cms (12 ins) long, which live in a dog's heart and the major blood vessels surrounding it. Dogs may have up to 200 worms. Symptoms may be loss of energy, loss of appetite, coughing, the development of a pot belly and anaemia.

Heartworms are transmitted by mosquitoes. The mosquito drinks the blood of an infected dog and takes in larvae with the blood. The larvae, called microfilaria, develop within the body of the mosquito and are passed on to the next dog bitten after the larvae mature. It takes two to three weeks for the larvae to develop to the infective stage within the body of the mosquito. Dogs should be treated at about six weeks of age, and maintained on a prophylactic dose given monthly.

Blood testing for heartworms is not necessarily indicative of how seriously your dog is infected. This is a dangerous disease. Although heartworm is a problem for dogs in America, Australia, Asia and Central Europe, dogs in the United Kingdom are not currently affected by heartworm.

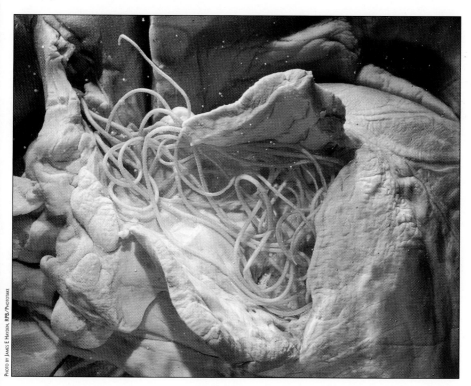

The heart of a dog infected with canine heartworm, *Dirofilaria immitis.*

HOMEOPATHY:
an alternative to conventional medicine

'Less is Most'

Using this principle, the strength of an homeopathic remedy is measured by the number of serial dilutions that were undertaken to create it. The greater the number of serial dilutions, the greater the strength of the homeopathic remedy. The potency of a remedy that has been made by making a dilution of 1 part in 100 parts (or 1/100) is 1c or 1cH. If this remedy is subjected to a series of further dilutions, each one being 1/100, a more dilute and stronger remedy is produced. If the remedy is diluted in this way six times, it is called 6c or 6cH. A dilution of 6c is 1 part in 1,000,000,000,000. In general, higher potencies in more frequent doses are better for acute symptoms and lower potencies in more infrequent doses are more useful for chronic, long-standing problems.

CURING OUR DOGS NATURALLY

Holistic medicine means treating the whole animal as a unique, perfect living being. Generally, holistic treatments do not suppress the symptoms that the body naturally produces, as do most medications prescribed by conventional doctors and vets. Holistic methods seek to cure disease by regaining balance and harmony in the patient's environment. Some of these methods include use of nutritional therapy, herbs, flower essences, aromatherapy, acupuncture, massage, chiropractic and, of course, the most popular holistic approach, homeopathy.

Homeopathy is a theory or system of treating illness with small doses of substances which, if administered in larger quantities, would produce the symptoms that the patient already has. This approach is often described as 'like cures like.' Although modern veterinary medicine is geared toward the 'quick fix,' homeopathy relies on the belief that, given the time, the body is able to heal itself and return to its natural, healthy state.

Choosing a remedy to cure a problem in our dogs is the difficult part of homeopathy. Consult with your veterinary surgeon for a professional diagnosis of your dog's symptoms. Often these symptoms require immediate conventional care. If your vet is willing, and knowledgeable, you may attempt an homeopathic remedy. Be aware that cortisone prevents homeopathic remedies from working. There are hundreds of possibilities and combinations to cure many problems in dogs, from basic physical problems such as excessive moulting, fleas or other parasites, unattractive doggy odour, bad breath, upset tummy, obesity, dry, oily or dull coat, diarrhoea, ear problems or eye discharge (including tears and dry or mucousy matter), to behavioural abnormalities, such as fear of loud noises, habitual licking, poor appetite, excessive barking and various phobias. From alumina to zincum metallicum, the remedies span the planet and the imagination…from flowers and weeds to chemicals, insect droppings, diesel smoke and volcanic ash.

Using 'Like to Treat Like'

Unlike conventional medicines that suppress symptoms, homeopathic remedies treat illnesses with small doses of substances that, if administered in larger quantities, would produce the symptoms that the patient already has. While the same homeopathic remedy can be used to treat different symptoms in different dogs, here are some interesting remedies and their uses.

Apis Mellifica
(made from honey bee venom) can be used for allergies or to reduce swelling that occurs in acutely infected kidneys.

Diesel Smoke
can be used to help control travel sickness.

Calcarea Fluorica
(made from calcium fluoride, which helps harden bone structure) can be useful in treating hard lumps in tissues.

Natrum Muriaticum
(made from common salt, sodium chloride) is useful in treating thin, thirsty dogs.

Nitricum Acidum
(made from nitric acid) is used for symptoms you would expect to see from contact with acids, such as lesions, especially where the skin joins the linings of body orifices or openings such as the lips and nostrils.

Symphytum
(made from the herb Knitbone, *Symphytum officianale*) is used to encourage bones to heal.

Urtica Urens
(made from the common stinging nettle) is used in treating painful, irritating rashes.

HOMEOPATHIC REMEDIES FOR YOUR DOG

Symptom/Ailment	Possible Remedy
ALLERGIES	Apis Mellifica 30c, Astacus Fluviatilis 6c, Pulsatilla 30c, Urtica Urens 6c
ALOPAECIA	Alumina 30c, Lycopodium 30c, Sepia 30c, Thallium 6c
ANAL GLANDS (BLOCKED)	Hepar Sulphuris Calcareum 30c, Sanicula 6c, Silicea 6c
ARTHRITIS	Rhus Toxicodendron 6c, Bryonia Alba 6c
CATARACT	Calcarea Carbonica 6c, Conium Maculatum 6c, Phosphorus 30c, Silicea 30c
CONSTIPATION	Alumina 6c, Carbo Vegetabilis 30c, Graphites 6c, Nitricum Acidum 30c, Silicea 6c
COUGHING	Aconitum Napellus 6c, Belladonna 30c, Hyoscyamus Niger 30c, Phosphorus 30c
DIARRHOEA	Arsenicum Album 30c, Aconitum Napellus 6c, Chamomilla 30c, Mercurius Corrosivus 30c
DRY EYE	Zincum Metallicum 30c
EAR PROBLEMS	Aconitum Napellus 30c, Belladonna 30c, Hepar Sulphuris 30c, Tellurium 30c, Psorinum 200c
EYE PROBLEMS	Borax 6c, Aconitum Napellus 30c, Graphites 6c, Staphysagria 6c, Thuja Occidentalis 30c
GLAUCOMA	Aconitum Napellus 30c, Apis Mellifica 6c, Phosphorus 30c
HEAT STROKE	Belladonna 30c, Gelsemium Sempervirens 30c, Sulphur 30c
HICCOUGHS	Cinchona Deficinalis 6c
HIP DYSPLASIA	Colocynthis 6c, Rhus Toxicodendron 6c, Bryonia Alba 6c
INCONTINENCE	Argentum Nitricum 6c, Causticum 30c, Conium Maculatum 30c, Pulsatilla 30c, Sepia 30c
INSECT BITES	Apis Mellifica 30c, Cantharis 30c, Hypericum Perforatum 6c, Urtica Urens 30c
ITCHING	Alumina 30c, Arsenicum Album 30c, Carbo Vegetabilis 30c, Hypericum Perforatum 6c, Mezerium 6c, Sulphur 30c
KENNEL COUGH	Drosera 6c, Ipecacuanha 30c
MASTITIS	Apis Mellifica 30c, Belladonna 30c, Urtica Urens 1m
PATELLAR LUXATION	Gelsemium Sempervirens 6c, Rhus Toxicodendron 6c
PENIS PROBLEMS	Aconitum Napellus 30c, Hepar Sulphuris Calcareum 30c, Pulsatilla 30c, Thuja Occidentalis 6c
PUPPY TEETHING	Calcarea Carbonica 6c, Chamomilla 6c, Phytolacca 6c
TRAVEL SICKNESS	Cocculus 6c, Petroleum 6c

Recognising a Sick Dog

Unlike colicky babies and cranky children, our canine charges cannot tell us when they are feeling ill. Therefore, there are a number of signs that owners can identify to know that their dogs are not feeling well.

Take note for physical manifestations such as:

- unusual, bad odour, including bad breath
- excessive moulting
- wax in the ears, chronic ear irritation
- oily, flaky, dull haircoat
- mucous, tearing or similar discharge in the eyes
- fleas or mites
- mucous in stool, diarrhoea
- sensitivity to petting or handling
- licking at paws, scratching face, etc.

Keep an eye out for behavioural changes as well including:

- lethargy, idleness
- lack of patience or general irritability
- lack of appetite, digestive problems
- phobias (fear of people, loud noises, etc.)
- strange behaviour, suspicion, fear
- coprophagia
- more frequent barking
- whimpering, crying

Get Well Soon

You don't need a DVR or a BVMA to provide good TLC to your sick or recovering dog, but you do need to pay attention to some details that normally wouldn't bother him. The following tips will aid Fido's recovery and get him back on his paws again:

- Keep his space free of irritating smells, like heavy perfumes and air fresheners.
- Rest is the best medicine! Avoid harsh lighting that will prevent your dog from sleeping. Shade him from bright sunlight during the day and dim the lights in the evening.
- Keep the noise level down. Animals are more sensitive to sound when they are sick.

- Be attentive to any necessary temperature adjustments. A dog with a fever needs a cool room and cold liquids. A bitch that is whelping or recovering from surgery will be more comfortable in a warm room, consuming warm liquids and food.
- You wouldn't send a sick child back to school early, so don't rush your dog back into a full routine until he seems absolutely ready.

Number-One Killer Disease in Dogs: CANCER

In every age, there is a word associated with a disease or plague that causes humans to shudder. In the 21st century, that word is 'cancer.' Just as cancer is the leading cause of death in humans, it claims nearly half the lives of dogs that die from a natural disease as well as half the dogs that die over the age of ten years.

Described as a genetic disease, cancer becomes a greater risk as the dog ages. Veterinary surgeons and dog owners have become increasingly aware of the threat of cancer to dogs. Statistics reveal that one dog in every five will develop cancer, the most common of which is skin cancer. Many cancers, including prostate, ovarian and breast cancer, can be avoided by spaying and neutering our dogs by the age of six months.

Early detection of cancer can save or extend your dog's life, so it is absolutely vital for owners to have their dogs examined by a qualified veterinary surgeon or oncologist immediately upon detection of any abnormality. Certain dietary guidelines have also proven to reduce the onset and spread of cancer. Foods based on fish rather than beef, due to the presence of Omega-3 fatty acids, are recommended. Other amino acids such as glutamine have significant benefits for canines, particularly those breeds that show a greater susceptibility to cancer.

Cancer management and treatments promise hope for future generations of canines. Since the disease is genetic, breeders should never breed a dog whose parents, grandparents and any related siblings have developed cancer. It is difficult to know whether to exclude an otherwise healthy dog from a breeding programme, as the disease does not manifest itself until the dog's senior years.

RECOGNISE CANCER WARNING SIGNS

Since early detection can possibly rescue your dog from becoming a cancer statistic, it is essential for owners to recognise the possible signs and seek the assistance of a qualified professional.

- Abnormal bumps or lumps that continue to grow
- Bleeding or discharge from any body cavity
- Persistent stiffness or lameness
- Recurrent sores or sores that do not heal
- Inappetence
- Breathing difficulties
- Weight loss
- Bad breath or odours
- General malaise and fatigue
- Eating and swallowing problems
- Difficulty urinating and defecating

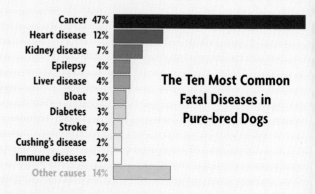

Cancer	47%
Heart disease	12%
Kidney disease	7%
Epilepsy	4%
Liver disease	4%
Bloat	3%
Diabetes	3%
Stroke	2%
Cushing's disease	2%
Immune diseases	2%
Other causes	14%

The Ten Most Common Fatal Diseases in Pure-bred Dogs

WELSH TERRIER

The term *old* is a qualitative term. For dogs, as well as for their masters, old is relative. Certainly we can all distinguish between a puppy Welsh Terrier and an adult Welsh Terrier—there are the obvious physical traits, such as size, appearance and facial expressions, and personality traits. Puppies and young dogs like to play with children. Children's natural exuberance is a good match for the seemingly endless energy of young dogs. They like to run, jump, chase and retrieve. When dogs grow older and cease their interaction with children, they are often thought of as being too old to keep pace with the kids. On the other hand, if a Welsh Terrier is only exposed to older people or quieter lifestyles, his life will normally be less active and the decrease in his activity level as he ages will not be as obvious.

If people live to be 100 years old, dogs live to be 20 years old. While this might seem like a good rule of thumb, it is very inaccurate. When trying to compare dog years to human years, you cannot make a generalisation about all dogs. Fortunately the Welsh Terrier, like most of his terrier brethren, is a long-lived dog that can live in good health for 12 to 15 years.

Although the Welsh Terrier tends to mature as early as one year of age, dogs generally are considered physically mature at around three years of age. On this basis, many theorise that the first three years of a dog's life are like seven times that of comparable humans. That means a 3-year-old dog is like a 21-year-old human. As the curve of comparison shows, there is no hard and fast rule for comparing dog and human ages. Small breeds, including the terriers, tend to live longer than large breeds; some breeds' adolescent periods last longer than others'; and some breeds experience rapid periods of growth. The comparison is made even more difficult, for, likewise, not all humans age at the same rate...and human females live longer than human males.

WHAT TO LOOK FOR IN SENIORS

Most veterinary surgeons and behaviourists use the seven-year mark as the time to consider a dog a 'senior' or 'veteran.' Neither term implies that the dog is geriatric and has begun to fail in mind and body. Ageing is essentially a slowing process. Humans readily admit that they feel a difference in their activity level from age 20 to 30, and then from 30 to 40, etc. By treating the seven-year-old dog as a senior, owners are able to implement certain therapeutic and preventative medical strategies with the help of their veterinary surgeons.

A senior-care programme should include at least two veterinary visits per year and screening sessions to determine the dog's health status, as well as nutritional counselling. Veterinary surgeons determine the senior dog's health status through a blood smear for a complete blood count, serum chemistry profile with electrolytes, urinalysis, blood pressure check, electrocardiogram, ocular tonometry (pressure on the eyeball) and dental prophylaxis.

Such an extensive programme for senior dogs is well advised before owners start to see the obvious physical signs of ageing, such as slower and inhibited movement, greying, increased sleep/nap periods and disinterest in play and other activity. This preventative programme promises a longer, healthier life for the ageing dog. Among the physical problems common in ageing dogs are the loss of sight and hearing, arthritis, kidney and liver failure, diabetes mellitus, heart disease and Cushing's disease (an hormonal disease).

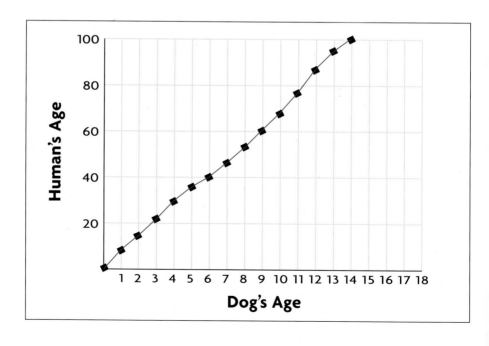

CDS: COGNITIVE DYSFUNCTION SYNDROME
'OLD-DOG SYNDROME'

There are many ways to evaluate old-dog syndrome. Veterinary surgeons have defined CDS (cognitive dysfunction syndrome) as the gradual deterioration of cognitive abilities. These are indicated by changes in the dog's behaviour. When a dog changes its routine response, and maladies have been eliminated as the cause of these behavioural changes, then CDS is the usual diagnosis.

More than half the dogs over eight years old suffer from some form of CDS. The older the dog, the more chance it has of suffering from CDS. In humans, doctors often dismiss the CDS behavioural changes as part of 'winding down.'

There are four major signs of CDS: the dog has frequent toilet accidents inside the home, sleeps much more or much less than normal, acts confused and fails to respond to social stimuli.

SYMPTOMS OF CDS

FREQUENT TOILET ACCIDENTS
- *Urinates in the house.*
- *Defecates in the house.*
- *Doesn't signal that he wants to go out.*

SLEEP PATTERNS
- *Moves much more slowly.*
- *Sleeps more than normal during the day.*
- *Sleeps less during the night.*

CONFUSION
- *Goes outside and just stands there.*
- *Appears confused with a faraway look in his eyes.*
- *Hides more often.*
- *Doesn't recognise friends.*
- *Doesn't come when called.*
- *Walks around listlessly and without a destination.*

FAILS TO RESPOND TO SOCIAL STIMULI
- *Comes to people less frequently, whether called or not.*
- *Doesn't tolerate petting for more than a short time.*
- *Doesn't come to the door when you return home.*

In addition to the physical manifestations discussed, there are some behavioural changes and problems related to ageing dogs. Dogs suffering from hearing or vision loss, dental discomfort or arthritis can become aggressive. Likewise, the near-deaf and/or blind dog may be startled more easily and react in an unexpectedly aggressive manner. Seniors suffering from senility can become more impatient and irritable. Housesoiling accidents are associated with loss of mobility, kidney problems and loss of sphincter control as well as plaque accumulation, physiological brain changes and reactions to medications. Older dogs, just like young puppies, suffer from separation anxiety, which can lead to excessive barking, whining, housesoiling and destructive behaviour. Seniors may become fearful of everyday sounds, such as vacuum cleaners, heaters, thunder and passing traffic. Some dogs have difficulty sleeping, due to discomfort, the need for frequent toilet visits and the like.

Owners should avoid spoiling the older dog with too many fatty treats. Obesity is a common problem in older dogs and subtracts years from their lives. Keep the senior dog as trim as possible, since excessive weight puts additional stress on the body's vital organs. Some breeders recommend supplementing the diet with foods high in fibre and lower in calories. Adding fresh vegetables and marrow broth to the senior's diet makes a tasty, low-calorie, low-fat supplement. Vets also offer speciality diets for senior dogs that are worth exploring.

Your dog, as he nears his twilight years, needs your patience and good care more than ever. Never punish an older dog for an accident or abnormal behaviour. For all the years of love, protection and companionship that your dog has provided, he deserves special attention and courtesies. The older dog may need to relieve himself at 3 a.m. because he can no longer hold it for eight hours. Older dogs may

SENIOR SIGNS

An old dog starts to show one or more of the following symptoms:

- The hair on the face and paws starts to turn grey. The colour breakdown usually starts around the eyes and mouth.

- Sleep patterns are deeper and longer, and the old dog is harder to awaken.

- Food intake diminishes.

- Responses to calls, whistles and other signals are ignored more and more.

- Eye contact does not evoke tail wagging (assuming it once did).

> ## NOTICING THE SYMPTOMS
> The symptoms listed below are symptoms that gradually appear and become more noticeable. They are not life-threatening; however, the symptoms below are to be taken very seriously and warrant a discussion with your veterinary surgeon:
>
> - Your dog cries and whimpers when he moves, and he stops running completely.
>
> - Convulsions start or become more serious and frequent. The usual convulsion (spasm) is when the dog stiffens and starts to tremble, being unable or unwilling to move. The seizure usually lasts for 5 to 30 minutes.
>
> - Your dog drinks more water and urinates more frequently. Wetting and bowel accidents take place indoors without warning.
>
> - Vomiting becomes more and more frequent.

not be able to remain crated for more than two or three hours. It may be time to give up a sofa or chair to your old friend. Although he may not seem as enthusiastic about your attention and petting, he does appreciate the considerations you offer as he gets older.

Your Welsh Terrier does not understand why his world is slowing down. Owners must make their dogs' transition into their golden years as pleasant and rewarding as possible.

WHAT TO DO WHEN THE TIME COMES

You are never fully prepared to make a rational decision about putting your dog to sleep. It is very obvious that you love your Welsh Terrier or you would not be reading this book. Putting a beloved dog to sleep is extremely difficult. It is a decision that must be made with your veterinary surgeon. You are usually forced to make the decision when your dog experiences one or more life-threatening symptoms that have become serious enough for you to seek medical (veterinary) help.

If the prognosis of the malady indicates that the end is near and that your beloved pet will only continue to suffer and experience no enjoyment for the balance of its life, then euthanasia is the right choice.

WHAT IS EUTHANASIA?

Euthanasia derives from the Greek, meaning *good death*. In other words, it means the planned, painless killing of a dog suffering from a painful, incurable condition, or who is so aged that it cannot walk, see, eat or control its excretory functions. Euthanasia is usually accomplished by injection with an overdose of anaesthesia or a barbiturate. Aside from the prick of the needle, the experience is usually painless.

MAKING THE DECISION

The decision to euthanise your dog is never easy. The days during which the dog becomes ill and the end occurs can be unusually stressful for you. If this is your first experience with the death of a loved one, you may need the comfort dictated by your religious beliefs. If you are the head of the family and have children, you should have involved them in the decision of putting your Welsh Terrier to sleep. Usually your dog can be maintained on drugs for a few days in order to give you ample time to make a decision. During this time, talking with members of your family or with people who have lived through the same experience can ease the burden of your inevitable decision.

THE FINAL RESTING PLACE

Dogs can have some of the same privileges as humans. The remains of your beloved dog can be buried in a pet cemetery, which is generally expensive. Alternatively, your dog can be cremated individually and the ashes returned to you. A less expensive option is mass cremation, although, of course, the ashes cannot then be returned. Vets can usually arrange the cremation on your behalf. The cost of these options should always be discussed frankly and openly with your veterinary surgeon. In Britain, if your dog has died at the surgery, the vet legally cannot allow you to take your dog's body home, because laws prohibit the burial of animals in home gardens.

GETTING ANOTHER DOG?

The grief of losing your beloved dog will be as lasting as the grief of losing a human friend or relative. In most cases, if your dog died of old age (if there is such a thing), it had slowed down considerably. Do you want a new Welsh Terrier puppy to replace it? Or are you better off finding a more mature Welsh Terrier, say two to three years of age, which will usually be house-trained and will have an already developed personality. In this case, you can find out if you like each other after a few hours of being together.

The decision is, of course, your own. Do you want another Welsh Terrier or perhaps a different breed so as to avoid comparison with your beloved friend? Most people usually buy the same breed because they know (and love) the characteristics of that breed. Then, too, they often know people who have the same breed and perhaps they are lucky enough that one of their friends expects a litter soon. What could be better?

Showing Your
WELSH TERRIER

When you purchase your Welsh Terrier, you will make it clear to the breeder whether you want one just as a loveable companion and pet, or if you hope to be buying a Welsh Terrier with show prospects. No reputable breeder will sell you a young puppy and tell you that it is *definitely* of show quality, for so much can go wrong during the early months of a puppy's development. If you plan

INFORMATION ON CLUBS
You can get information about dog shows from kennel clubs and breed clubs:

Fédération Cynologique Internationale
14, rue Leopold II, B-6530 Thuin, Belgium
www.fci.be

The Kennel Club
1-5 Clarges St., Piccadilly, London W1Y 8AB
UK
www.the-kennel-club.org.uk

American Kennel Club
5580 Centerview Dr., Raleigh, NC 27606-3390
USA
www.akc.org

Canadian Kennel Club
89 Skyway Ave., Suite 100, Etobicoke,
Ontario
M9W 6R4 Canada
www.ckc.ca

to show, what you will hopefully have acquired is a puppy with 'show potential.'

To the novice, exhibiting a Welsh Terrier in the show ring may look easy, but it takes a lot of hard work and devotion to do top winning at a show such as the prestigious Crufts Dog Show, not to mention a little luck too!

The first concept that the canine novice learns when watching a dog show is that each dog first competes against members of its own breed. Once the judge has selected the best member of each breed (Best of Breed), provided that the show is judged on a Group system, that chosen dog will compete with other dogs in its group. Finally, the best of each group will compete for Best in Show.

The second concept that you must understand is that the dogs are not actually compared against one another. The judge compares each dog against its breed standard, which is the written description of the ideal specimen of the breed. While some early breed standards were indeed based on specific dogs that were famous or popular, many dedicated enthusiasts say that a perfect

The win of wins in Britain—-Best in Show at Crufts. Ch Saredon Forever Young took the prestigious show's top honours in 1998. Owned by Dave Scawthorn and Judy Averis (pictured).

specimen, as described in the standard, has never walked into a show ring, has never been bred and, to the woe of dog breeders around the globe, does not exist. Breeders attempt to get as close to this ideal as possible with every litter, but theoretically the 'perfect' dog is so elusive that it is impossible. (And if the 'perfect' dog were born, breeders and judges would never agree that it was indeed 'perfect.')

If you are interested in exploring the world of dog showing, your best bet is to join your local breed club. These clubs often host both Championship and Open Shows, and sometimes Match meetings and special events, all of which could be of interest, even if you are only an onlooker. Clubs also send out newsletters, and some organise training days and seminars in order that people may learn more

about their chosen breed. To locate the breed club closest to you, contact The Kennel Club, the ruling body for the British dog world. The Kennel Club governs not only conformation shows but also working trials, obedience shows, agility trials and field trials. The Kennel Club furnishes the rules and regulations for all of these events plus general dog registration and other basic requirements of dog ownership. Its annual show, called the Crufts Dog Show, held in Birmingham, is the largest benched show in England. Every year over 20,000 of the UK's best dogs qualify to participate in this marvellous show, which lasts four days.

The Kennel Club governs many different kinds of shows in Great Britain, Australia, South Africa and beyond. At the most competitive and prestigious of these shows, the Championship Shows, a dog can earn Challenge Certificates (CCs), and thereby become a Show Champion or a Champion. A dog must earn three CCs under three different judges to earn the prefix of 'Sh Ch' or 'Ch.' Some breeds must also qualify in a field trial in order to gain the title of full Champion, though the Welsh Terrier is not one such breed. CCs are awarded to a very small percentage of the dogs competing, and dogs that are already Champions compete with others for these coveted CCs. The number of CCs awarded in any one year is based upon the total number of dogs in each breed entered for competition.

There are three types of Championship Shows: an all-breed General Championship Show for all Kennel-Club-recognised breeds; a Group Championship Show, which is limited to breeds within one of the groups; and a Breed Show, which is usually confined to a single breed. The Kennel Club determines which breeds at which Championship Shows will have the opportunity to earn CCs (or tickets). Serious exhibitors often will opt not to participate if the tickets are withheld at a particular show. This policy makes earning championships even more difficult to accomplish.

Open Shows are generally less competitive and are frequently used as 'practice shows' for young dogs. There are hundreds of Open Shows each year that can be delightful social events and are great first show experiences for the novice. Even if you're considering just watching a show to wet your paws, an Open Show is a great choice.

While Championship and Open Shows are most important for the beginner to understand, there are other types of shows in which the interested dog owner can participate. Training clubs sponsor Matches that can be entered on the day of the show for a nominal fee. In these introductory-level exhibitions, two dogs' names are pulled out of a hat and 'matched,' the winner of that match goes on to the next round and eventually only one dog is left undefeated.

Exemption Shows are much more light-hearted affairs with usually only four pedigree classes and several 'fun' classes, all of which can be entered on the day of the show. Exemption Shows are sometimes held in conjunction with small agricultural shows and the proceeds must be given to a charity. Limited Shows are also available in small number. Entry is restricted to members of the club that hosts the show, although you can usually join the club when making an entry.

Before you actually step into the ring, you would be well advised to sit back and observe the judge's ring procedure. If it is your first time in the ring, do not be over-anxious and run to the front of the line. It is much better to stand back and study how the exhibitor in front of you is performing. The judge asks each handler to 'stand' the dog, hopefully showing the dog off to his best advantage. The judge will observe the dog from a distance and from different angles, and approach the dog to check his teeth, overall structure, alertness and muscle tone, as well as consider how well the dog 'conforms' to the standard. Most importantly, the judge will have the exhibitor move the dog around the ring in some pattern that he or she should specify (another advantage to not going first, but always listen since some judges change their directions—and the judge is always right!). Finally, the judge will give the dog one last look before moving on to the next exhibitor.

If you are not in the top three at your first show, do not be discouraged. Be patient and consistent, and you may eventually find yourself in the winning line-up. Remember that the winners were once in your shoes and have devoted many hours and much money to earn the placement. If you find that your dog is losing every time and never getting a nod, it may be time to consider a different dog sport or to just enjoy your Welsh Terrier as a pet.

Virtually all countries with a recognised speciality breed club (sometimes called a 'parent' club) offer show conformation competition specifically for and among Welsh Terriers. Under direction of the club, other special events for hunting, tracking, obedience, agility and earthdog activities may be offered as well, whether for titling or just for fun.

EARTHDOG TESTS

Clubs in many countries run earthdog tests for all the small terriers and Dachshunds, using artificial dens and fully protected prey animals. In these and other countries, the Welsh Terrier is felt to be an excellent natural hunter and therefore is the chosen breed for this pursuit. In the 16th century, 'jingles' or bell collars were put on the dogs as a mild protection from being bitten, but primarily as a scare tactic to bolt the fox. These bells proved to have another very useful purpose: they served as an aid in locating a dog

Left: A tunnel is hardly an obstacle for this athletic Welsh Terrier in an agility trial. **Right:** Flying high! This agile Welsh clears a jump gracefully with room to spare.

stuck underground. Today, modern locating devices are used to track dogs that need to be dug out.

The American Kennel Club in the United States promotes earthdog trials for Welsh Terriers, and the dogs have proved to be exceptional in these pursuits. Similarly, instinct tests are popular among the show set, and many of the handsome, professionally groomed Welsh Terriers also prove what they are made of underneath their beguiling exteriors.

WORKING TRIALS

Working trials can be entered by any well-trained dog of any breed, not just Gundogs or Working dogs. Many dogs that earn the Kennel Club Good Citizen Dog award choose to participate in a working trial. There are five stakes at both Open and Championship levels: Companion Dog (CD), Utility Dog (UD), Working Dog (WD), Tracking Dog (TD) and Patrol Dog (PD). As in conformation shows, dogs compete against a standard and, if the dog reaches the qualifying mark, it obtains a certificate. The exercises are divided into groups, and the dog must achieve at least 70 percent of the allotted score for each exercise in order to qualify. If the dog achieves 80 percent in the Open level, it receives a Certificate of Merit (COM); in the Championship level, it receives a Qualifying Certificate. At the CD stake, dogs must participate in four groups: Control, Stay, Agility and Search (Retrieve and Nosework). At the next three levels, UD, WD and TD, there are only three groups: Control, Agility and Nosework.

To earn the UD, WD and TD, dogs must track approximately one-half mile for articles laid from one-half hour to three hours previously. Tracks consist of turns and legs, and fresh ground is used for each participant. The fifth stake, PD, involves teaching manwork, which is not recommended for every breed.

AGILITY TRIALS

Agility trials began in the United Kingdom in 1977 and have since spread around the world, especially to the United States, where they are very popular. The handler directs his dog over obstacle courses that include jumps (such as those used in the working trials), as well as tyres, the dog walk, weave poles, pipe tunnels, collapsed tunnels, etc. The Kennel Club requires that dogs not be trained for agility until they are 12 months old. This dog sport is great fun for dog and owner, and interested owners should join a training club that has obstacles and experienced agility handlers who can introduce you and your dog to the 'ropes' (and tyres, tunnels, etc.).

FÉDÉRATION CYNOLOGIQUE INTERNATIONALE

Established in 1911, the Fédération Cynologique Internationale (FCI) represents the 'world kennel club.' This international body brings uniformity to the breeding, judging and showing of pure-bred dogs. Although the FCI originally included only five European nations: France, Germany, Austria, the Netherlands and Belgium (which remains its headquarters), the organisation today embraces nations on six continents and recognises well over 300 breeds of pure-bred dog.

FCI sponsors both national and international shows. The hosting country determines the judging system and breed standards are always based on the breed's country of origin. Dogs from every country can participate in these impressive canine spectacles, the largest of which is the World Dog Show, hosted in a different country each year.

There are three titles attainable through the FCI: the International Champion, which is the most prestigious; the International Beauty Champion, which is based on aptitude certificates in different countries; and the International Trial Champion, which is based on achievement in obedience trials in different countries. The title of Champion at an FCI show requires a dog to win three CACs (*Certificats d'Aptitude au Championnat*), at regional or club shows under three different judges who are breed specialists. The title of International Champion is gained by winning four CACIBs (*Certificats d'Aptitude au Championnat International de Beauté*), which are offered only at international shows, with at least a one-year lapse between the first and fourth award.

The FCI is divided into ten groups. At the World Dog Show, the following classes are offered for each breed: Puppy Class (6–9 months), Youth Class (9–18 months), Open Class (15 months or older) and Champion Class. A dog can be awarded a classification of Excellent, Very Good, Good, Sufficient and Not Sufficient. Puppies can be awarded classifications of Very Promising, Promising or Not Promising. Four placements are made in each class. After all classes for dogs and bitches are judged, a Best of Breed is selected. Other special groups and classes may also be shown. Each exhibitor showing a dog receives a written evaluation from the judge.

Besides the World Dog Show and other all-breed shows, you can exhibit your dog at speciality shows held by different breed clubs. Speciality shows may have their own regulations.

Behaviour of Your
WELSH TERRIER

As a Welsh Terrier owner, you have selected your dog so that you and your loved ones can have a companion, a protector, a friend and a four-legged family member. You invest time, money and effort to care for and train the family's new charge. Of course, this chosen canine behaves perfectly! Well, perfectly like a *dog*.

THINK LIKE A DOG

Dogs do not think like humans, nor do humans think like dogs, though we try. Unfortunately, a dog is incapable of comprehending how humans think, so the responsibility falls on the owner to adopt a proper canine mindset. Dogs cannot rationalise, and dogs exist in the present moment. Many dog owners make the mistake in training of thinking that they can reprimand their dog for something he did a while ago. Basically, you cannot even reprimand a dog for something he did 20 seconds ago! Either catch him in the act or forget it! It is a waste of your and your dog's time—in his mind, you are reprimanding him for whatever he is doing at that moment.

The following behavioural problems represent some which owners most commonly encounter. Every dog is unique and every situation is unique. No author could purport for you to solve your Welsh Terrier's problems simply by reading a script. Here we outline some basic 'dogspeak' so that owners' chances of solving behavioural problems are increased.

Discuss bad habits with your veterinary surgeon and he/she can recommend a behavioural specialist to consult in appropriate cases. Since behavioural abnormalities are the main reason for owners' abandoning their pets, we hope that you will make a valiant effort to solve your Welsh Terrier's problems. Patience and understanding are virtues that must dwell in every pet-loving household.

SEPARATION ANXIETY

Recognised by behaviourists as the most common form of stress for dogs, separation anxiety can also lead to destructive behaviours in your dog. It's more than your Welsh Terrier's howling

'Are you home yet?' A dog left home alone all day will often anxiously await his owner's return.

his displeasure at your leaving the house and his being left alone. This is a normal reaction, no different from the child who cries as his mother leaves him on the first day at school. Separation anxiety is more serious. In fact, if you are constantly with your dog, he will come to expect you with him all of the time, making it even more traumatic for him when you are not there.

Obviously, you enjoy spending time with your dog, and he thrives on your love and attention. However, it should not become a dependent relationship in which he is heartbroken without you. This broken heart can also bring on destructive behaviour as well as loss of appetite, depression and lack of interest in play and interaction. Canine behaviourists have been spending much time and energy to help owners better understand the significance of this stressful condition.

One thing you can do to minimise separation anxiety is to make your entrances and exits as low-key as possible. Do not give your dog a long drawn-out goodbye, and do not lavish him with hugs and kisses when you return. This is giving in to the attention that he craves, and it will only make him miss it more when you are away. Another thing you can try is to give your dog a treat when you leave; this will not only keep him occupied and keep his mind off the fact that you have just left, but it will also help him associate your leaving with a pleasant experience.

You may have to accustom your dog to being left alone at intervals. Of course, when your dog starts whimpering as you approach the door, your first instinct will be to run to him and comfort him, but do not do it! Really—eventually he will adjust to your absence. His anxiety stems from being placed in an unfamiliar situation; by familiarising him with being alone, he will learn that he will survive. That is not to say you should purposely leave your dog home alone, but the dog needs to know that, while he can depend on you for his care, you do not have to be by his side 24 hours a day. Some behaviourists recommend tiring the dog out before you leave home—take him for a good long walk or engage in a game of fetch in the garden.

When the dog is alone in the house, he should be placed in his crate—another distinct advantage to crate training your dog. The crate should be placed in his familiar happy family area, where he normally sleeps and already feels comfortable, thereby making him feel more at ease when he is alone. Be sure to give the dog a special chew toy to enjoy while he settles into his crate.

AGGRESSION

This is a problem that concerns all responsible dog owners. Aggression can be a very big problem in dogs, and, when not controlled, always becomes dangerous. An aggressive dog, no matter the size, may lunge at, bite or even attack a person or another dog. Aggressive behaviour is not to be tolerated. It is more than just inappropriate behaviour; it is painful for a family to watch their dog become unpredictable in his behaviour to the point where they are afraid of him. While not all aggressive behaviour is dangerous, growling, baring teeth, etc., can be frightening. It is important to ascertain why the dog is acting in this manner. Aggression is a display of dominance, and the dog should not have the dominant role in its pack, which is, in this case, your family.

It is important not to challenge an aggressive dog, as

DID YOU KNOW?
Dogs get to know each other by sniffing each other's backsides. It seems that each dog has a telltale odour, probably created by the anal glands. It also distinguishes sex and signals when a female will be receptive to a male's attention. Some dogs snap at another dog's intrusion of their private parts.

this could provoke an attack. Observe your Welsh Terrier's body language. Does he make direct eye contact and stare? Does he try to make himself as large as possible: ears pricked, chest out, tail erect? Height and size signify authority in a dog pack—being taller or 'above' another dog literally means that he is 'above' in social status. These body signals tell you that your Welsh Terrier thinks he is in charge, a problem that needs to be addressed. An aggressive dog is unpredictable; you never know when he is going to strike and what he is going to do. You cannot understand why a dog that is playful one minute is growling the next.

Fear is a common cause of aggression in dogs. Perhaps your Welsh Terrier had a negative experience as a puppy, which causes him to be fearful when a similar situation presents itself later in life. The dog may act aggressively in order to protect himself from whatever is making him afraid. It is not always easy to determine what is making your dog fearful, but if you can isolate what brings out the fear reaction, you can help the dog get over it.

Supervise your Welsh Terrier's interactions with people and other dogs, and praise the dog when it goes well. If he starts to act aggressively in a situation, correct him and remove him from the situation. Do not let people approach the dog and start petting him without your express permission. That way, you can have the dog sit to accept petting, and praise him when he behaves properly. You are focusing on praise and on modifying his behaviour by rewarding him when he acts appropriately. By being gentle and by supervising his interactions, you are showing him that there is no need to be

> **DOGGIE DEMOCRACY**
> Your dog inherited the pack-leader mentality. He only knows about pecking order. He instinctively wants to be 'top dog,' but you have to convince him that you are boss. There is no such thing as living in a democracy with your dog. You are the one who makes the rules.

afraid or defensive.

The best solution is to consult a behavioural specialist, one who has experience with terriers or specifically with the Welsh Terrier, if possible. Together, perhaps you can pinpoint the cause of your dog's aggression and do something about it. An aggressive dog cannot be trusted, and a dog that cannot be trusted is not safe to have as a family pet. If, very unusually, you find that your pet has become untrustworthy and you feel it necessary to seek a new home with a more suitable family and environment, explain fully to the new owners all your reasons for rehoming the dog to be fair to all concerned. In the very worst case, you will have to consider euthanasia.

AGGRESSION TOWARD OTHER DOGS

A dog's aggressive behaviour toward another dog stems from not enough exposure to other dogs at an early age. If other dogs make your Welsh Terrier nervous and agitated, he will lash out as a protective mechanism. A dog that has not received sufficient exposure to other canines tends to think that he is the only dog on the planet. The animal becomes so dominant that he does not even show signs that he is fearful or threatened. Without growling or any other physical signal as a warning, he will lunge at and bite the other dog. A way to correct this is to let your Welsh Terrier approach another dog when walking on lead. Watch very closely and, at the first sign of aggression, correct your Welsh Terrier and pull him away. Scold him for any sign of discomfort, and then praise him when he ignores the other dog. Keep this up until either he stops the aggressive behaviour, learns to ignore other dogs or even accepts other dogs. Praise him lavishly for this correct behaviour.

DOMINANT AGGRESSION

A social hierarchy is firmly established in a wild dog pack. The dog wants to dominate those under him and please those above him. Dogs know that there must be a leader. If you are not the obvious choice for emperor, the dog will assume the throne! These conflicting innate desires are what a dog owner is up against when he sets about training a dog. In training a dog to obey commands, the owner is reinforcing that he is the top dog in the 'pack' and that the dog should, and should want to, serve his superior. Thus, the owner is suppressing the dog's urge to dominate by modifying his behaviour and making him obedient.

An important part of training is taking every opportunity to reinforce that you are the leader. The simple action of making your Welsh Terrier sit to wait for his food instead of allowing him to run up to get it when he wants it says that you control when he eats; he is dependent on you for food. Although it may be difficult, do not give in to your dog's wishes every time he whines or looks at you with pleading eyes. It is a constant effort to show the dog that his place in the pack is at the bottom. This is not meant to sound cruel or inhumane. You love your Welsh Terrier and you should treat him with care and affection. You (hopefully) did not get a dog just so you could control

Properly socialised dogs should show neither fear nor aggression toward other dogs that they meet. This Welsh Terrier and German Shepherd dog are pleased to make each other's acquaintance.

another creature. Dog training is not about being cruel or feeling important, it is about moulding the dog's behaviour into what is acceptable and teaching him to live by your rules. In theory, it is quite simple: catch him in appropriate behaviour and reward him for it. Add a dog into the equation and it becomes a bit more trying, but as a rule of thumb, positive reinforcement is what works best.

With a dominant dog, punishment and negative reinforcement can have the opposite effect of what you are after. It can make a dog fearful and/or act out aggressively if he feels he is being challenged. Remember, a dominant dog perceives himself at the top of the social heap, and will fight to defend his perceived status. The best way to prevent that is to never give him reason to think that he is in control in the first place. If you are having trouble training your Welsh Terrier and it seems as if he is constantly challenging your authority, seek the help of an obedience trainer or behavioural specialist. A professional will work with both you and your dog to teach you effective techniques to use at home. Beware of trainers who rely on excessively harsh methods; scolding is necessary now and then, but the focus in your training should always be on positive reinforcement.

> **DID YOU KNOW?**
> Punishment is rarely necessary for a misbehaving dog. Dogs that habitually behave badly probably had a poor education and do not know what is expected of them. They need training. Negative reinforcement on your part usually does more harm than good.

SEXUAL BEHAVIOUR
Dogs exhibit certain sexual behaviours that may have influenced your choice of male or female when you first purchased your Welsh Terrier. To a certain extent, spaying/neutering will eliminate these behaviours, but if you are purchasing a dog that you wish to breed from, you should be aware of what you will have to deal with throughout the dog's life.

Female dogs usually have two oestruses per year, with each season lasting about three weeks. These are the only times in which a female dog will mate, and she usually will not allow this until the second week of the cycle, although this varies from bitch to bitch. If not bred during the heat cycle, it is not uncommon for a bitch to experience a false pregnancy, in which her mammary glands swell and she exhibits maternal tendencies toward toys or other objects.

With male dogs, owners must be

aware that whole dogs (dogs who are not neutered) have the natural inclination to mark their territory. Males mark their territory by spraying small amounts of urine as they lift their legs in a macho ritual. Marking can occur both outdoors in the garden and around the neighbourhood as well as indoors on furniture legs, curtains and the sofa. Such behaviour can be very frustrating for the owner; early training is strongly urged before the 'urge' strikes your dog. Neutering the male at an appropriate early age can solve this problem before it becomes a habit.

Other problems associated with males are wandering and mounting. Both of these habits, of course, belong to the unneutered dog, whose sexual drive leads him away from home in search of the bitch in heat. Males will mount females in heat, as well as any other dog, male or female, that happens to catch their fancy. Other possible mounting partners include his owner, the furniture, guests to the home and strangers on the street. Discourage such behaviour early on.

Owners must further recognise that mounting is not merely a sexual expression but also one of dominance, which can be exhibited in dogs and bitches alike. Be consistent and be persistent, and you will find that you can 'move mounters.'

CHEWING

The national canine pastime is chewing, and Welsh Terriers have lots of tooth enamel to spare! Every dog loves to sink his 'canines' into a tasty bone, but sometimes that bone is in his owner's hand! Dogs need to chew, to massage their gums, to make their new teeth feel better and to exercise their jaws. This is a natural behaviour that is deeply embedded in all things canine. Our role as owners is not to stop the dog's chewing, but rather to redirect it to positive, chew-worthy objects. Be an informed owner and purchase proper chew toys, like strong nylon bones, that will not splinter. Be sure that the objects are safe and durable, since your dog's safety is at risk. Again, the owner is responsible for ensuring a dog-proof environment.

The best answer is prevention; that is, put your shoes, handbags and other tasty objects in their

Always keep an eye on what your pup puts in his mouth. This pup has chosen a stick over his array of plush toys, which could prove dangerous.

proper places (out of the reach of the growing canine mouth). Direct puppies to their toys whenever you see them 'tasting' the furniture legs or the leg of your trousers. Make a loud noise to attract the pup's attention and immediately escort him to his chew toy and engage him with the toy for at least four minutes, praising and encouraging him all the while. An array of safe, interesting chew toys will keep your dog's mind and teeth occupied, and distracted from chewing on things he shouldn't.

Some trainers recommend deterrents, such as hot pepper, a bitter spice or a product designed for this purpose, to discourage the dog from chewing unwanted objects. Test these products to see which works best before investing in large quantities.

DIGGING

Digging, which is seen as a destructive behaviour to humans, is actually quite a natural behaviour in dogs. If ever a dog was meant to dig, the Welsh Terrier was bred to do the job. However, he is not an offender unless moles or voles live in your garden, in which case the Welsh may actually prove beneficial to your lawn and so have your forgiveness for any divots incurred in the process.

As earthdogs, Welsh Terriers are not the indiscriminate diggers one might expect. Some individuals will go at it like Welsh miners, but by and large they save their digging prowess purely for going after vermin. Although terriers are most associated with digging, any dog's desire to dig can be irrepressible and most frustrating to his owners.

When digging occurs in your garden, it is actually a normal behaviour redirected into something the dog can do in his everyday life. In the wild, a dog would be actively seeking food, making his own shelter, etc. He would be using his paws in a purposeful manner for his survival. Since you provide him with food and shelter, he has no need to use his paws for these purposes, and so the energy that he would be using may manifest itself in the form of little holes all over your garden and flower beds.

Perhaps your dog is digging as a reaction to boredom—it is somewhat similar to someone eating a whole bag of crisps in front of the TV—because they are there and there is nothing better to do! Basically, the answer is to provide the dog with adequate play and exercise so that his mind and paws are occupied, and so that he feels as if he is doing something useful.

Of course, digging is easiest to control if it is stopped as soon as possible, but it is often hard to catch a dog in the act. If your dog is a compulsive digger and is not easily distracted by other activities, you can designate an area on your property where he is allowed to dig. If you catch him digging in an off-limits area of the garden, immediately bring him to the approved area and praise him for digging there. Keep a close eye on him so that you can catch him in the act—that is the only way to make him understand what is permitted and what is not. If you take him to an hole he dug an hour ago and tell him 'No,' he will understand that you are not fond of holes, or dirt or flowers. If you catch him while he is stifle-deep in your tulips, that is when he will get your message.

JUMPING UP

Jumping up is a dog's friendly way of saying hello! Some dog owners do not mind when their dog jumps up. The problem arises when guests come to the house and the dog greets them in the same manner—whether they like it or not! However friendly the greeting may be, the chances are that your visitors will not appreciate your dog's enthusiasm. The dog will not be able to distinguish upon whom he can jump and whom he cannot. Therefore, it is probably best to discourage this behaviour entirely.

Pick a command such as 'Off' (avoid using 'Down' since you will use that for the dog to lie down) and tell him 'Off' when he jumps up. Place him on the ground on all fours and have him sit, praising him the whole time. Always lavish him with praise and petting when he is in the sit position. In this way, you can give him a warm affectionate greeting, let him know that you are as excited to see him as he is to see you and instil good manners at the same time!

BARKING

Dogs cannot talk—oh, what they would say if they could! Instead, barking is a dog's way of 'talking.' It can be somewhat frustrating because it is not always easy to tell what a dog means by his bark—is he excited, happy, frightened or angry? Whatever it is that the dog is trying to say, he should not be punished for barking. It is only when the barking becomes excessive, and when the excessive barking becomes a bad habit, that

BARKING STANCE

Did you know that a dog is less likely to bark when sitting than standing? Watch your dog the next time that you suspect he is about to start barking. You'll notice that as he does, he gets up on all four feet. Hence, when teaching a dog to stop barking, it helps to get him to sit before you command him to be quiet.

the behaviour needs to be modified.

Fortunately, Welsh Terriers are not as vocal as most other dogs; they tend to use their barks more purposefully. If an intruder came into your home in the middle of the night and your Welsh Terrier barked a warning, wouldn't you be pleased? You would probably deem your dog a hero, a wonderful guardian and protector of the home. On the other hand, if a friend drops by unexpectedly, rings the doorbell and is greeted with a sudden sharp bark, you would probably be annoyed at the dog. But in reality, isn't this just the same behaviour? The dog does not know any better. Unless he sees who is at the door and it is someone he knows, he will bark as a means of vocalising that his (and your) territory is being threatened. While your friend is not posing a threat, it is all the same to the dog. Barking is his means of letting you know that there is an intrusion, whether friend or foe, on your property. This type of barking is instinctive and should not be discouraged.

Excessive habitual barking, however, is a problem that should be corrected early on. As your Welsh Terrier grows up, you will be able to tell when his barking is purposeful and when it is for no reason. You will become able to distinguish your dog's different barks and their meanings. For

You won't believe where your Welsh will stick his nose when food is concerned! Stop a potential thief by leaving nothing 'stealable' within your dog's reach.

> ## PROFESSIONAL TRAINING
> If your dog barks menacingly or growls at strangers, or if he growls at anyone who comes near his food while he is eating, playing with a toy or taking a rest in his favourite spot, he needs proper professional training because sooner or later this behaviour can result in someone being bitten.

example, the bark when someone comes to the door will be different from the bark when he is excited to see you. It is similar to a person's tone of voice, except that the dog has to rely totally on tone of voice because he does not have the benefit of using words. An incessant barker will be evident at an early age.

There are some things that encourage a dog to bark. For example, if your dog barks non-stop for a few minutes and you give him a treat to quieten him, he believes that you are rewarding

him for barking. He will associate barking with getting a treat and will keep doing it until he is rewarded. On the other hand, if you give him a command such as 'Quiet' and praise him after he has stopped barking for a few seconds, he will get the idea that being 'quiet' is what you want him to do.

FOOD STEALING

Is your dog devising ways of stealing food from your coffee table or kitchen counter? If so, you must answer the following questions: Is your Welsh Terrier hungry, or is he 'constantly famished' like many dogs seem to be? Face it, some dogs are more food-motivated than others. They are totally obsessed by the smell of food and can only think of their next meal. Food stealing is terrific fun and always yields a great reward—FOOD, glorious food.

Your goal as an owner, therefore, is to be sensible about where food is placed in the home and to reprimand your dog whenever he is caught in the act of stealing. But remember, only reprimand your dog if you actually see him stealing, not later when the crime is discovered; that will be of no use at all and will only serve to confuse him.

BEGGING

Just like food stealing, begging is a favourite pastime of hungry puppies! It achieves that same

'What's for lunch?' Has your Welsh taken a place at the head of the table? If so, you need to stand your ground in enforcing the 'no-begging' laws.

lovely result—FOOD! Dogs quickly learn that their owners keep the 'good food' for themselves, and that we humans do not dine on dried food alone. Begging is a conditioned response related to a specific stimulus, time and place. The sounds of the kitchen, cans and bottles opening, crinkling bags, the smell of food in preparation, etc., will excite the dog, and soon the paws will be in the air!

Here is the solution to stopping this behaviour: Never give in to a beggar! You are rewarding the dog for sitting pretty, jumping up, whining and rubbing his nose into you by giving him food. By ignoring the dog, you will (eventually) force the behaviour into extinction. Note that the behaviour is likely to get worse before it disappears, so be sure there are not any 'softies' in the family who will give in to little 'Oliver' every time he whimpers, 'More, please.'

My Welsh Terrier

PUT YOUR PUPPY'S FIRST PICTURE HERE

Dog's Name _____

Date _____ Photographer _____